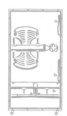

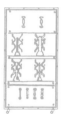
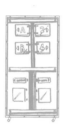

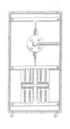

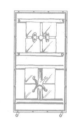

FUSION

Nicholas Grimshaw & Partners ■ Industrial Design

We would like to thank our friend
and mentor Rainer Kranz of Mabeg
for his continued support of the
Industrial Design department,
and for his inspiration and help in
making the exhibition possible.

Introduction 6

The text is taken from a discussion between Nicholas Grimshaw, Duncan Jackson and Eoin Billings of the NGP Industrial Design department, and an Industrial Design student, Christopher Bell who has been working with Nicholas Grimshaw and Partners. January 23, 1998.

Chris *My first question for you Nick is to ask you why, when people know you as an architect, do you have 'industrial design' as one of the services on your letter head.*

Nick Well, first of all I should say that I see the joint between industrial design and architecture as a seamless one. We have 'industrial design' on our letter head because we recognise its value as an essential part of the creative process and part of the way this practice works. We are encouraging a cross-fertilization of ideas about materials and processes which, in turn, leads to better solutions.

Chris *Is this usual amongst architectural practices ?*

Nick I can't speak for other practices, but we have found that Duncan and Eoin have been able to form strong links with manufacturers and this has been invaluable in our architectural practice. There are obvious advantages in architects not continually reinventing the wheel. Establishing an information base of industrial design details as an in-house resource for architects working in the practice has helped us to avoid this.

Chris *You give your industrial designers great scope and freedom. How does this work in terms of their relationship with you and the company ?*

Nick Well, I think this freedom is very important. Although Duncan heads up our industrial design department , he and Eoin can develop products in their own right. I trust them to keep me fully informed and to discuss with me whether any project or product should be their own or be part of Nicholas Grimshaw and Partners.

Chris Why did you call this exhibition "Fusion"?

Nick An important part of the way we work is to collaborate closely with all those involved in getting buildings built. The more we share knowledge and experience the further the industry will progress. The exhibition is intended to give an insight into the way we work and "Fusion" was chosen to convey the importance of collaboration. The word fusion also has the great advantage in that it means the same thing in many languages. The dictionary gives this as the English meaning; "a fusing or melting together, a blending, coalition."

I hope too, that the exhibition will be inspirational for those connected with what we do, and to students like yourself who want to work in this field.

Chris Is this why the exhibition is so geared for travel ?

Duncan: Exactly. And that's why we have constructed flight cases in which to display these production processes. If you like, it's a very "travel friendly" exhibition !

You know, too, that our suppliers are all over Europe. So, as well as making the invisible processes visible to as many people as possible, the exhibition also reflects the diverse sources of our materials and our suppliers. In fact, nearly all our exhibitors will be supporting the exhibition in their own countries.

Chris Where did the idea for completely self-contained exhibition flight cases originally come from?

Nick We have always shipped architectural models around the world in flight cases. It seemed a natural step to use this tried and tested technology to move the exhibition about. The idea of using the flight case as the display case itself is similar to the way in which travelling cabin trunks used to open up into wardrobes. With castors on the bottom, and with built in lighting, the whole thing becomes a self-contained mobile show. It can go anywhere; be wheeled in, plugged in, and open to the public within hours.

Duncan It's also a product in itself. Mabeg's Profile One is the display system used within the cases. In addition, Zumbtobel, another exhibitor, worked with us to develop a lighting solution for illuminating the exhibits. The exhibition case is a good example of developing a solution to a specific problem and ending up with a product. We take advantage of opportunities like these while working on architectural projects.

Chris *Why would people visiting the show be interested in the manufacturing processes?*

Nick I remember many years ago going around the Ford Factory at Dagenham. They have thousands of visitors a year from all walks of life and everybody, but everybody, was interested in the process of the car going together. People are constantly confronted by objects which are cast, extruded, fired or folded and I think they will be fascinated by understanding the actual processes by which they are made. I think visitors will be really curious.

We are showing stages which people don't usually see. Fusion offers new insight into how things are made and how they go together. We show how molten metal is poured into sand moulds to make a seat. We show how materials are extruded and stamped, and we show many of the final products.

Eoin I'm sure the exhibition will be of interest to students of both design and architecture. Many that I have spoken to were very curious about what we have done and how we achieved it. The exhibition responds to their interest.

Duncan For example, Chris, your recent visit to an aluminium extrusion plant is crucial to your understanding of the material and the process. That one visit has completely changed your perception of how you can work with aluminium.

Chris What's the significance of architectural projects within this exhibition?

Nick The architectural project gives the broader context through which industrial design solutions can be better understood. Waterloo International Terminal, for example, was much admired for its industrial design detail. Clients that have come to us to develop a new product recognised this. I believe Waterloo also demonstrates how working closely with manufacturers makes it possible to achieve both practical and beautiful solutions to difficult problems.

Chris I can see how Waterloo is relevant but can you explain why the cladding from the Chippenham Building is?

Nick Whilst basic, Chippenham is a genuine example of a component building in the Prouvé tradition. We took a standard fixing system and developed a series of cladding panels which specifically met the client's need for flexibility. As a result the panels and windows and doors could all be interchanged.

Chris Why not just use standard systems?

Nick I think the point here is that sites vary enormously in terms of the climate affecting them and the influences surrounding them. Also the physical requirements of a warehouse are very different from those for an office building. We feel it is wrong and often very wasteful to use a standard solution in all situations. Cladding systems in the

United States for example are used in both Boston and Atlanta without alteration. This is wasteful because there is inherent redundancy in a solution that can deal with these extremes of climate. We look at the whole environment of the building. Just as a building solution is different in London or Seville so a bus shelter would be very different in Madrid or Stockholm.

Another example is the Western Morning News which is a single glazed solution. There is no need for insulated double glazing when you have a print machine in the building running 24 hours a day. You actually want to lose heat.

Chris Is it different working with manufacturers developing products as opposed to designing a building?

Nick Well no, not really. For instance, Mabeg's interest in us was based on the way we solved the detail problems at Waterloo. This building convinced them that we could develop a sophisticated product range in a very competitive market. I think the disciplines and sensitivities required when designing a building are the same when developing a product. Both involve structure, space and skin.

Dieser Text basiert auf einer Diskussion zwischen
Nicholas Grimshaw, Duncan Jackson und Eoin
Billings aus der NGP Industrial Design Abteilung, und
Christopher Bell, einem Industrial Design Studenten,
der bei Nicholas Grimshaw & Partners arbeitet.
23. Januar 1998.

Chris *Meine erste Frage an Sie, Herr Grimshaw, ist warum Sie 'Industrial Design' als eine Ihrer Dienstleistungen auf Ihrem Briefkopf anbieten, obwohl Sie als Architekt bekannt sind.*

Nick Also, zuerst müßte ich sagen, daß für mich die Verbindung zwischen Industrial Design und Architektur nahtlos ist. Auf unserem Briefkopf steht 'Industrial Design' weil wir es als wertvollen, sogar unentbehrlichen, Teil des kreativen Vorgangs anerkennen, und teilweise funktioniert dieses Verfahren recht gut. Wir unterstützen das Zusammenspiel von Ideen, Werkstoffen und Herstellungsverfahren, die dann zu besseren Lösungen führen.

Chris *Ist so etwas üblich in Architekturbüros?*

Nick Über andere Büros kann ich mich nicht äußern, aber wir haben die Erfahrung gemacht, daß Duncan und Eoin enge Beziehungen mit Herstellern geformt haben, und dies hat einen unschätzbaren Beitrag zu unserer Architektur ergeben. Natürlich ist es nich sehr vorteilhaft, wenn Architekten immer wieder das Rad neu erfinden. Wir haben dies vermieden indem wir eine Datenbank von Industrial Design Details eingerichtet haben, von der die Architekten im Büro als in-house Hilfsmittel Gebrauch machen.

Chris *Sie erlauben Ihren Industrial Designern viel Bewegungsfreiheit. Wie funktioniert das hinsichtlich ihrer Beziehung zu Ihnen und zum Büro?*

Nick Ich denke; daß Freiheit sehr wichtig ist. Obwohl Duncan unsere Industrial Design Abteilung leitet, können er und Eoin trotzdem Ihre eigenen Produkte entwickeln. Ich vertraue ihnen, daß sie mich standig informiert halten, und daß Sie mit mir besprechen, ob ein Produkt ihr eigenes oder ein Teil von Nicholas Grimshaw & Partners sein sollte.

Chris *Warum nennen Sie diese Ausstellung 'Fusion'?*

Nick Ein wichtiger Teil unserer Arbeitsmethoden ist die nahe Zusammenarbeit mit allen, die am Bauvorgang beteiligt sind. Je mehr wir Wissen und Erfahrung teilen, desto weiter wird die Industrie fortschreiten. Die Ausstellung beabsichtigt, einen Einblick in unsere Arbeitsmethoden zu vermitteln, und der Name 'Fusion' wurde gewählt, um die Wichtigkeit von Zusammenarbeit zu übermitteln. Das Wort 'Fusion' hat weiterhin den großen Vorteil, dass es die gleiche Bedeutung in vielen Sprachen hat. In Englisch wird es im Wörterbuch folgenderweise definiert: 'eine Vermischung oder Verschmelzung; eine Vereinigung'.

Ich hoffe auch, daß die Ausstellung für alle anregend ist die eine Verbindung zu unserer Arbeit haben, insbesondere für Studenten wie Sie selbst, die in diesem Feld arbeiten wollen.

Chris *Ist das der Grund warum die Ausstellung so auf Reisen ausgerichtet ist?*

Duncan Genau. Deshalb haben wir Flugcontainer konstruiert, in denen wir diese Produktionsvorgänge zur Schau stellen können. Man konnte sagen, daß dies eine sehr 'reisefreundliche' Ausstellung ist!

Chris *Woher kam die Idee für vollkommen selbststandige Ausstellungscontainer?*

Nick Wir haben schon immer Architekturmodelle in Flugcontainern in die ganze Welt verschickt. Es war ein natürlicher Schritt, diese erprobte und zuverlässige Technologie anzuwenden, um die Ausstellung zu transportieren. Die Idee, die Flugcontainer selber als Schaukasten zu verwenden, ist Schrankkoffern ähnlich, die man zu Kleiderschränken öffnen konnte.

Mit Laufrollen und eingebauter Beleuchtung wird das ganze eine selbstständige, bewegliche Vorstellung. Sie kann überall hin; sie kann angefahren und eingestöpselt werden, und kann in wenigen Stunden der Öffentlichkeit zugänglich gemacht werden.

Duncan Die Ausstellung ist selbst ein Produkt. Das Ausstellunssystem, das wir in den Containern angewandt haben, ist Mabeg's Profile One. Zusätzlich hat Zumbtobel, ein anderer Aussteller, mit uns zusammengearbeitet um eine Beleuchtungsstrategie für die Ausstellungsstücke zu entwickeln. Die Schaukästen sind ein gutes Beispiel einer Lösung zu einem bestimmten Problem, die dann zu einem Produkt führt. Wir nutzen solche auch Gelegenheiten während wir an Architekturprojekten arbeiten.

Chris *Warum sollten sich die Besucher zu dieser Ausstellung an Herstellungsverfahren interessieren?*

Nick Ich erinnere mich, wie ich vor vielen Jahren die Ford Fabrik in Dagenham besichtigt habe. Die Fabrik empfängt jedes Jahr tausende von Besuchern aus allen Schichten und Berufen, und alle waren sehr daran interessiert, wie Autos zusammengebaut werden. Wir werden ständig mit gegoßenen, stranggepreßten, gebrannten oder gepfalzten Objekten konfrontiert, und ich glaube, daß es sie faszinieren würde, die Verfahren, mit denen diese Objekte hergestellt wurden, zu verstehen. Ich glaube, daß die Besucher neugierig sein werden. Wir zeigen

Herstellungsstufen die normalerweise nicht gesehen werden. Fusion bietet einen Einblick in die Herstellung und Montage von normalen Gegenständen. Wir zeigen wie geschmolzenes Metall in Gußformen aus Sand geschüttet wird um einen Sitz zu machen. Wir zeigen wie Wekstoffe extrudiert und gestanzt werden, und wir zeigen viele der Endprodukte.

Eoin Ich bin mir sicher, daß die Ausstellung sowohl Design– als auch Architekturstudenten interessieren wird. Viele Leute mit denen ich mich unterhalten habe waren sehr interessiert an unserer Arbeit, und wie wir sie zustande bringen können. Diese Ausstellung geht auf ihr Interesse ein.

Duncan Zum Beispiel, Chris, Ihr Besuch letztens zu einem Betrieb in dem Aluminium extrudiert wird war entscheidend für Ihr Verständnis des Werkstoffes und der Verfahren. Dieser eine Besuch hat Ihre Empfindung für Aluminium als Material vollstandig verändert.

Chris Was ist die Bedeutung der Architekturprojekte in dieser Ausstellung?

Nick Architekturprojekte bieten einen weitreichenderen Zusammenhang in dem die Industrial Design Lösungen besser verstanden werden können. Waterloo International Terminal, zum Beispiel, wurde bewundert wegen seiner Industrial Design Details. Kunden, die zu uns gekommen sind, um ein neues Produkt zu entwickeln, haben dies erkannt. Ich glaube, daß Waterloo zeigt wie es möglich ist praktische und schöne Losungen zu schweren Problemen zu finden indem man mit Herstellern nah zusammenarbeitet.

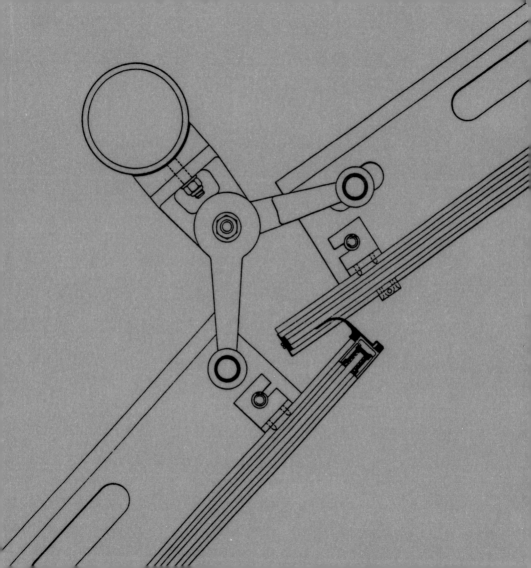

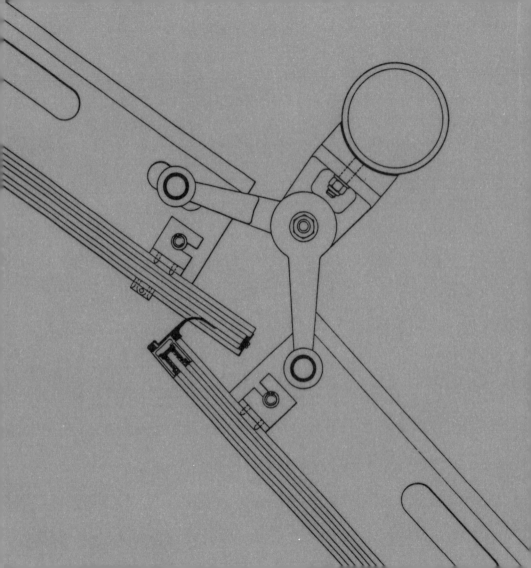

Chris Ich verstehe schon, warum Waterloo bedeutend ist,
aber warum ist die Verkleidung des Chippenham Gebäudes
wichtig?

Nick Chippenham ist zwar relativ einfach, aber es ist
ein wirkliches Beispiel eines Gebäudes aus Einzelteilen
in der Prouvé Tradition. Wir benutzten ein
Standardbefestigungssystem, und entwickelten eine Reihe
von Verkleidungsteilen die die ausdrückliche Forderung des
Bauherren für Flexibilität erfullten. Das Ergebnis war, daß
Fenster– und Turpaneele frei austauschbar waren.

Chris Warum habt ihr nicht ein Standardsystem benutzt?

Nick Zu dieser Frage muss ich erklären, daß sich
Standorte für Gebäude oft stark unterscheiden, hinsichtlich
Klima und anderer Einflüsse. Außerdem sind die physischen
Bedürfnisse eines Lagers und die eines Bürogebaudes
sehr verschieden. Wir denken, daß es falsch, und
oft sehr verschwenderisch ist, in allen Situationen
Standardlösungen anzuwenden. Verkleidungssysteme in
den Vereinigten Staaten, zum Beispiel, werden sowohl in
Boston als auch in Atlanta ohne Veränderungen angewandt.
Dies ist sehr verschwenderisch wegen der zwangsläufigen
Doppelfunktion einer Lösung die mit diesen beiden
klimatischen Extremen fertigwerden muß. Wir ziehen
die ganze Umgebung des Gebäudes in Erwägung.
Genau wie sich eine Gebäudestrategie in London von
einer in Seville unterscheidet, so müßte sich eine
Bushaltestellenuberdachung in Madrid von einer in
Stockholm unterscheiden.
   Ein weiteres Beispiel ist das einfach verglaste Western
Morning News Gebäude. Wärmegedämmte
Doppelverglasung ist nicht notwendig wenn man bedenkt,
dass die Druckmaschine im Gebaude 24 Stunden am Tag
läuft. Wärmeverlust ist sogar erwünscht.

Chris *Gibt es einen großen Unterschied zwischen dem*
Entwurf eines Gebäudes, und der Zusammenarbeit mit
Herstellern die Produkte entwickeln?

Nick Eigentlich nicht. Zum Beispiel, Mabeg's Interesse
an uns beruht auf der Art und Weise in der wir die
Detailprobleme bei Waterloo gelöst haben. Dieses
Gebäude hat sie überzeugt, daß wir imstande waren, eine
anspruchsvolle Produktreihe für einen Markt mit starker
Konkurrenz entwickeln zu können. Ich denke, daß das
gleiche Einfühlugsvermögen und die gleichen fachlichen
Fertigkeiten die für den Entwurf eines Gebäudes notwendig
sind auch für die Entwicklung eines Produktes angewandt
werden müssen. Beide betreffen Struktur, Raum und Haut.

El texto recoge una conversación entre Nicholas Grimshaw, Duncan Jackson y Eoin Billings del departamento de Diseño Industrial de NGP, y un estudiante de Diseño Industrial, Christopher Bell, que ha estado trabajando con Nicholas Grimshaw and Partners. 23 de enero de 1998.

Chris *Nick, lo primero que quiero preguntarte es ¿por qué, cuando la gente te conoce por arquitecto, aparece 'diseño industrial' como uno de los servicios en los membretes de tu oficina?*

Nick Bueno, en primer lugar quiero manifestar que veo al diseño industrial y a la arquitectura como una unión perfecta. Tenemos 'diseño industrial' en nuestro membrete porque reconocemos su valor como parte esencial del proceso creativo y como parte de la forma de trabajo de este estudio. Queremos promover un intercambio de ideas sobre materiales y procesos que nos lleve a encontrar soluciones mejores.

Chris *¿Es esto normal entre los estudios de arquitectura?*

Nick No puedo hablar por otros estudios, pero los fuertes lazos que Duncan y Eoin han formado con fabricantes han resultado inestimables para nuestra arquitectura. Hay ventajas obvias para un arquitecto en no estar constantemente reinventando la rueda. El establecer una base de información recogiendo los detalles de diseño industrial como un recurso propio para los arquitectos del estudio nos ha ayudado a evitar esto.

Chris *Le ofreces a tus Diseñadores Industriales grandes posibilidades y libertad. ¿Cómo funciona esto con respecto a su relación contigo y el estudio?*

Nick Bueno, pienso que esta libertad es muy importante. Aunque Duncan dirige nuestro departamento de diseño industrial, él y Eoin pueden desarrollar sus productos independientemente. Confío en ellos para mantenerme completamente informado y para tratar conmigo si cualquier proyecto o producto debería ser suyo o ser parte del trabajo de Nicholas Grimshaw and Partners.

Chris *¿Por qué le llamaste a esta exhibición 'Fusión'?*

Nick Una parte importante de nuestra manera de trabajar es la colaboración estrecha con todos aquellos relacionados en el proceso de construir edificios. Cuanto más compartamos los conocimientos y la experiencia más avanzará el sector. La exposición pretende dar una percepción de la manera en la que trabajamos y se eligió 'Fusión' para transmitir la importancia de esta colaboración. La palabra fusión también tiene la ventaja de que significa lo mismo en muchos idiomas. El diccionario da como significado de la palabra: "...una unión o fundición de partes, una mezcla, una coalición..." Espero también que la exposición inspire a esas personas relacionadas con lo que nosotros hacemos y a estudiantes como tú que quieren trabajar en este campo.

Chris *¿Es este el motivo por lo que la exposición está tan orientada al viaje?*

Nick Exactamente. Y por eso hemos construido cajones de embalaje en los que se presentan estos procesos de producción. Si te parece, ¡esta es una exposición muy 'amiga de viajar'!

También sabes que nuestros proveedores se encuentran por toda Europa. Así que, además de hacer visibles estos procesos invisibles para el mayor número de gente posible, la exposición también refleja las diversas fuentes de nuestros materiales y proveedores. De hecho, casi todos nuestros proveedores patrocinarán la exposición en su propio país.

Chris *¿De dónde surgió la idea de cajones de embalaje completamente independientes?*

Nick Siempre hemos enviado por todo el mundo maquetas arquitectónicas en cajones de embalaje. Parecía un paso natural utilizar esta tecnología, ya probada, para desplazar la exposición de un lado para otro. La idea de usar el cajón de embalaje como vitrina de exposición en sí es similar a la manera en que los antiguos baúles de viaje al abrirse se convertían en armarios. Con ruedecitas en la parte inferior, y con iluminación empotrada, todo ello se convierte en una vitrina móvil independiente. Puede ir a cualquier lugar; se empuja a la sala, se enchufa y en pocas horas está abierta al público.

Duncan Es también un producto en sí. El 'Profile One' de Mabeg es el sistema empleado dentro de los cajones. Además, Zumbtobel, otro expositor, trabajó con nosotros para desarrollar una solución integrada para la iluminación de los objetos expuestos. El cajón de exposición es un buen ejemplo de desarrollo de una solución específica a un problema que resulta en un producto. Aprovechamos oportunidades como esta mientras trabajamos en proyectos de arquitectura.

Chris *¿Por qué habría de interesarse la gente que visita la exposición en los procesos de fabricación?*

Nick Recuerdo andar por la Fábrica de Ford en Dagenham hace muchos años. Tienen miles de visitantes al año, gente de todas las profesiones y condiciones sociales, y todos, absolutamente todos, estaban interesados en el proceso de cómo se monta un coche. La gente se encuentra constantemente delante de objetos que están fundidos, extrudidos, cocidos o doblados y creo que se fascinarán cuando comprendan los procesos en sí por los que se fabrican. Pienso que los visitantes sentirán mucha curiosidad. Mostramos etapas que la gente normalmente no ve. "Fusion" ofrece una nueva perspectiva de cómo se fabrican las cosas y de qué forma se montan. Mostramos cómo se vierte el metal fundido en moldes de arena para hacer un asiento. Mostramos cómo se extruden y graban los materiales, y además mostramos muchos de los productos finales.

Eoin Estoy seguro de que la exposición será de interés para estudiantes tanto de diseño como de arquitectura. Muchos de ellos con los que he hablado sentían mucha curiosidad por lo que hemos hecho y cómo lo conseguimos. La exposición responde a este interés.

Duncan Por ejemplo, Chris, tu reciente visita a una planta de extrudir aluminio es crucial para tu entendimiento del material y del proceso. Una sola visita ha servido para cambiar completamente tu percepción de cómo puedes trabajar con el aluminio.

Chris *¿Cuál es la importancia de los proyectos de arquitectura en esta exposición?*

Nick El proyecto de arquitectura proporciona un contexto más amplio para poder entender mejor las soluciones de diseño industrial. Pongamos un ejemplo, se admiró mucho la Terminal Internacional de Waterloo por los detalles de su diseño industrial. Clientes que se han acercado a nosotros para desarrollar un nuevo producto reconocieron esto. Creo que Waterloo también demuestra cómo la estrecha colaboración con los fabricantes hace posible alcanzar soluciones a problemas difíciles que son al mismo tiempo prácticas y bellas.

Chris Veo por qué es relevante Waterloo, pero ¿puedes explicar por qué es relevante el revestimiento del Edificio Chippenham?

Nick Aún siendo básico, Chippenham es un ejemplo genuino de un edificio de componentes en la tradición de Prouvé. Cogimos un sistema de fijación estándar y desarrollamos una serie de paneles de revestimiento que satisfacían específicamente los requisitos de flexibilidad del cliente. Como resultado, los paneles y ventanas y puertas son todos intercambiables.

Chris ¿Por qué no utilizar un sistema estándar?

Nick Yo pienso que la clave aquí está en que los solares varían enormemente con respecto al clima que los afecta y a las influencias de su alrededor. También los requisitos físicos de un almacén son muy diferentes a los de un edificio de oficinas. Pensamos que está mal y que a menudo es poco económico utilizar una solución estándar en todas las situaciones. En los Estados Unidos, por ejemplo, utilizan sistemas de revestimiento tanto en Boston como en Atlanta sin alteración alguna. Esto es poco económico porque existe una redundancia inherente a la solución que puede acomodar estos extremos de clima. Nosotros estudiamos el medio ambiente global del edificio. Al igual que una solución arquitectónica es diferente en Londres o en Sevilla, también una marquesina sería muy diferente en Madrid o en Estocolmo.

Otro ejemplo es el edificio para el diario Western Morning News que utiliza una solución de acristalado sencillo. No hay necesidad de aislamiento por acristalado doble cuando tienes una imprenta en el edificio funcionando las 24 horas del día. Realmente lo que quieres es perder calor.

Chris *¿Es diferente trabajar con fabricantes desarrollando productos a trabajar con ellos para diseñar un edificio?*

Nick Pues no, en realidad no. Por ejemplo, el interés de Mabeg por nosotros se basó en nuestra forma de resolver los problemas de detalle en Waterloo. Este edificio les convenció de que nosotros podíamos desarrollar una sofisticada gama de productos en un mercado muy competitivo. Creo que las disciplinas y sensibilidades requeridas al diseñar un edificio son las mismas que para desarrollar un producto. Ambas implican estructura, espacio y envoltura.

Spanish manufacturers Cemusa commissioned Nicholas Grimshaw and Partners to design a new range of street furniture. The finished products demonstrate the successful partnership between designer and manufacturer.

The design is based around the concept of a kit of components which can be used in various combinations to achieve flexibility and continuity throughout the entire range.

The roof for the bus shelter in this range comprises individual glass panels and cast aluminium arms. A symmetrically extruded aluminium beam supplies all the fixing points to support either a double or single sided roof and accommodates all services. These include wire management, rainwater drainage and lighting. This integrated solution is particularly responsive to site specific installation problems.

A variety of configurations allows specifying local authorities the opportunity to customise the shelters and emphasise their regional identity.

Der spanische Hersteller Cemusa beauftragte Nicholas Grimshaw and Partners mit dem Entwurf einer neuen Art von Straßenmöbilierung. Das fertige Produkt zeugt von der erfolgreichen Partnerschaft zwischen Designer und Hersteller.

Das Design basiert auf einem Konzept eines Satzes von Bauteilen, die auf verschiedene Arten kombiniert werden können, was Flexibilität und Kontinuität innerhalb der gesamten Serie mit sich bringt.

Das Dach der Bushaltestelle in dieser Serie besteht aus individuellen Glaspaneelen und Aluminiumgußhalterungen. Ein symmetrisch extrudierter Aluminiumbalken bietet alle Fixierpunkte zur Anbringung des ein– oder zweiseitigen Daches und integrierten Versorgungsleitungen, einschließlich Verkabelung, Regenwasserabfluß und Beleuchtung. Dies integrierte System eignet sich besonders zur Lösung von ortsspezifischen Installationsproblemen.

Eine Vielzahl von Konfigurationen ermöglicht den auftragvergebenden Gemeinden, die individuelle Gestaltung der Haltestellen, und Betonung ihrer regionalen Identität.

El fabricante español Cemusa encargó a Nicholas Grimshaw & Partners el diseño de una nueva gama de mobiliario urbano. Los productos terminados demuestran la asociación con éxito entre el fabricante y el proyectista.

El diseño se basa en el concepto de un juego de componentes que se pueden utilizar en varias combinaciones para conseguir flexibilidad y continuidad a través de la gama completa.

La cubierta de la marquesina de autobús en esta.gama comprende paneles individuales de cristal con brazos de aluminio fundido. Una extrusión de aluminio simétrica ofrece todos los puntos de fijación para soportar tanto una cubierta sencilla como una doble, y acepta todos los servicios. Estos incluyen cableado estructurado, desagüe de aguas pluviales y alumbrado. Esta sulución integrada responde específicamente a los problemas específicos de instalación en su emplazamiento.

Una variedad de configuraciones ofrece a las autoridades locales licitantes la oportunidad de personalizar las marquesinas y resaltar su identidad regional.

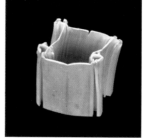

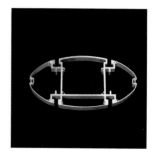

The completed bus shelter in Madrid,
with the first samples of the roof
beam extrusions.

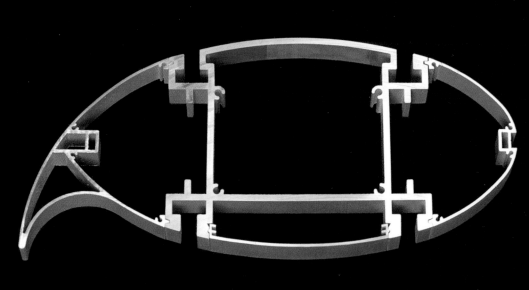

Bus shelter roof beam, double glazing
arm and corner assembly.

Bus stop prototype.
Extruded bus stop profile.

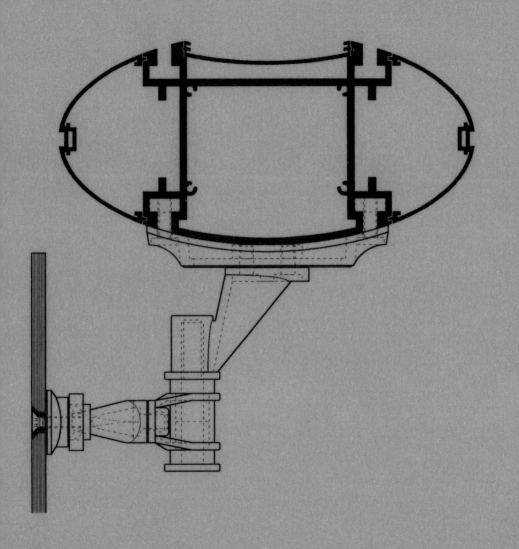

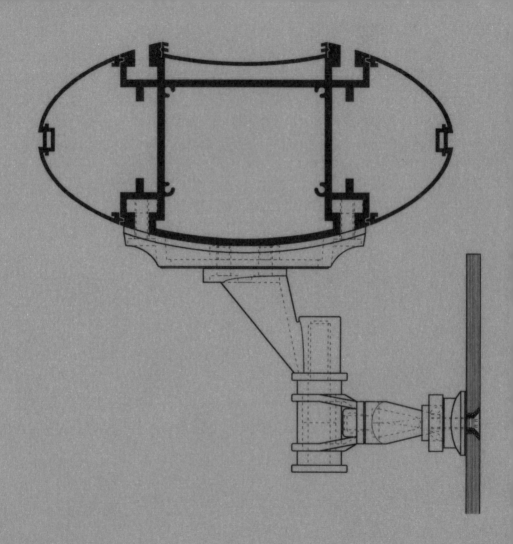

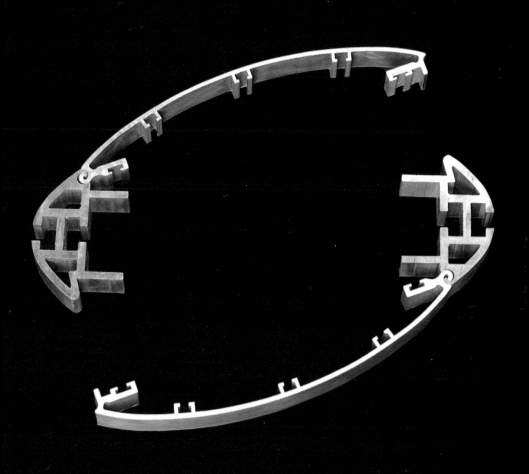

Flexible seating options are made possible by a kit of parts approach. The supporting beam can accommodate any combination of single or back to back seating modules. The beam can also function by itself as a perch.

There was close collaboration between Nicholas Grimshaw and Partners' designers and Cemusa's engineers. This enabled the pattern makers to make an MDF model of the seat directly from design drawings.

This model is used to create hard wax patterns for the casting process. The patterns can be replaced when they wear out using the original model. Detailed forms are pressed out in sand and filled with molten aluminium. The seats are then anodised to give added durability and texture.

The design for the sand-cast aluminium bus shelter seat refers to traditional Spanish forms and its height takes into consideration the requirements of the elderly and infirm.

Das Prinzip eines Bausatzes bestehend aus Einzelteilen ermöglicht flexibles Sitzen. Der Träger ist für jede beliebige Kombination von Einzel– oder Rücken-an-Rücken-Sitzmodulen geeignet. Der Träger selber kann auch alleinstehend als Sitzstange genutzt werden.

Die gute Zusammenarbeit zwischen den Designern von Nicholas Grimshaw and Partners und den Ingenieuren von Cemusa ermöglichte es den Modellschreinern, ein MDF Modell des Sitzes direkt vom Reißbrett herzustellen.

Dieses Modell wird dann zur Herstellung von Hartwachsmustern für den Gußprozeß genutzt. Die Modelle können bei Verschleiß mit Hilfe der Originalmodelle ersetzt werden. Detaillierte Formen werden in Sand gepreßt und mit geschmolzenem Aluminium gefüllt. Anschließend werden die Sitze anodisiert, wodurch sie zusätzliche Widerstandsfähigkeit und Struktur erhalten.

Das Design für den Sandgußaluminiumsitz der Bushaltestelle ist von traditionellen spanischen Formen abgeleitet; in seiner Höhe nimmt es Rücksicht auf die Bedürfnisse älterer und schwacher Menschen.

Un planteamiento de juegos de componentes permite opciones de asientos flexibles. La viga de soporte puede aceptar cualquier combinación de módulos de asientos individuales o dobles de respaldo contra respaldo. La viga también es capaz de funcionar por sí sola para apoyarse.

Hubo una estrecha colaboración entre los diseñadores de Nicholas Grimshaw & Partners y los ingenieros de Cemusa. Esto facilitó a los modelistas la creación de un prototipo en DM del asiento utilizando directamente los planos de diseño.

Se utiliza este modelo para crear moldes de cera sólida para el proceso de fundición. Los moldes pueden reemplazarse cuando se desgastan usando el prototipo original. Las formas detalladas son prensadas en arena y rellenadas con aluminio fundido. Después los asientos son anodizados para conseguir durabilidad y textura adicionales.

El diseño del asiento de la marquesina de autobús en aluminio fundido en arena se identifica con formas tradicionales españolas y su altura toma en cuenta las necesidades de los ancianos y enfermos.

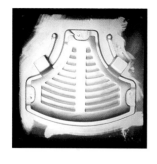  

Pattern, sand mould and
cast bus shelter seat.

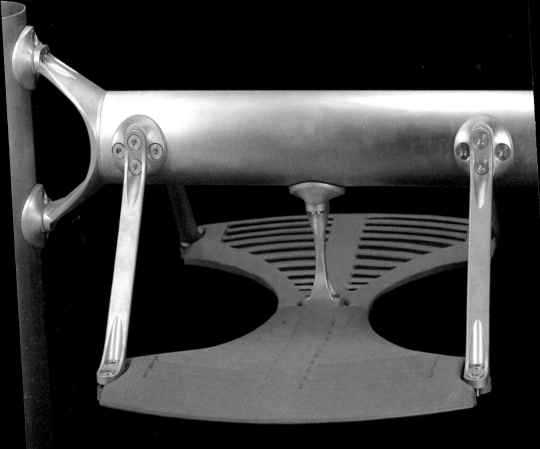

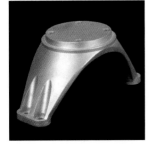
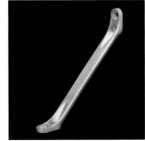

Seat assembly and components.

The highly engineered kit of parts which forms the core of this range of street furniture embodies much of the general design philosophy of Nicholas Grimshaw and Partners. A high specification standard product adaptable through a range of customised add-ons, minimises design obsolescence. It also maximises the long term economic benefits to both manufacturer and specifier. The quality of these components greatly reduces the need for costly on-site maintenance. Cemusa strongly believe that this initial investment is justified bearing in mind the lifespan of the product. The basic principle is that, where maintenance is necessary due to accident or damage, only the affected component need be replaced. This minimises costs as well as the time that the shelter is out of commission.

The franchise period for street furniture is often up to fifteen years, so recyclability has been an important consideration – these shelters can be relocated in several positions during their lifetime. The high specification and mutual compatibility of the components greatly helps to achieve a positive environmental impact.

Der hochwertige Einzelteilbausatz, der den Kern dieser Serie von Stadtmöbeln darstellt, verkörpert vieles der allgemeinen Designphilosophie von Nicholas Grimshaw and Partners. Ein hochwertiges Standardprodukt, das mit Hilfe einer Reihe von kundenspezifischen Zusätzen adaptiert werden kann minimiert die Designveralterung. Es maximiert außerdem die langfristigen wirtschaftlichen Vorteile für den Hersteller, sowie den Auftraggeber. Die Qualität der Komponenten reduziert den Bedarf an Vorortwartung erheblich. Cemusa ist davon überzeugt, daß die Ausgangsinvestition sich mit Hinblick auf die Produktlebensdauer lohnt. Das Grundprinzip hierbei ist, daß bei Wartungsbedarf als Folge von Unfall oder Schaden, ausschließlich die betroffenen Komponenten ausgetauscht werden müssen. Dies minimiert die Kosten, sowie die Zeitspanne, in der die Bushaltestelle nicht genutzt werden kann.

Der Franchising Zeitraum für Stadtmöbel erstreckt sich öfters auf fünfzehn Jahre, weswegen Wiederverwertbarkeit von erheblicher Bedeutung war – diese Haltestellen können während ihrer Lebensdauer an mehreren Orten aufgestellt werden. Die hohe Spezifikation und Kompatibilität der Komponenten hilft erheblich positive Umweltauswirkungen zu erzielen.

El juego de componentes con altas prestaciones de ingeniería que forma el núcleo de esta gama de mobiliario urbano comprende gran parte de la pauta general de diseño de Nicholas Grimshaw & Partners. Un producto estándar de alta especificación adaptable por toda una serie de componentes adicionales personalizados reduce al mínimo la obsolescencia del diseño. También potencia al máximo las ventajas económicas a largo plazo tanto para el fabricante como para el proyectista. La calidad de estos componentes reduce considerablemente la necesidad de mantenimiento costoso in situ. Cemusa cree firmemente que esta inversión inicial está justificada teniendo en cuenta la vida útil del producto. El principio básico es que, cuando el mantenimiento es necesario debido a accidente o daños, sólo el componente afectado necesita ser sustituido. Esto reduce al mínimo los costes y también reduce el tiempo que la marquesina está fuera de servicio.

El período de franquicia para el mobiliario urbano es a menudo hasta quince años, por ello la capacidad de reciclaje ha sido una consideración importante: estas marquesinas pueden ser reinstaladas en varias posiciones durante su vida útil. La alta especificación y compatibilidad mutua de estos componentes aporta una importante contribución a conseguir un impacto positivo medioambiental.

Key component, the 'saddle'.

Glazing components and assembly.

Roof beam to post connector,
prototype pattern and casting.

The arms which support the bus shelter glazing are manufactured using a lost wax, or investment casting process. Each and every component is made from an individual wax casting which is then melted or 'lost' during the next stage of production.

A soft aluminium negative is made from a single brass master. This is then filled with wax as many times as necessary to create individual patterns. Each of these is dipped in ceramic material which sets to form a mould. The wax is then melted out and the moulds filled with molten stainless steel to form the components.

Lost wax casting is a traditional technique and is still used today in the manufacture of hip replacement joints. The process is self-finishing and capable of greater accuracy than sand casting. This, along with the fact that stainless steel is long lasting and easily renovated, makes the process a very economical one.

Cemusa Lost Wax Stainless Steel Casting

Die Halterungen, die die Verglasung der Bushaltestelle tragen, werden mit Hilfe eines Wachsausschmelzguß-, oder Genaugußprozesses hergestellt. Jede einzelne Komponente wird aus einem individuellen Wachsguß hergestellt, der dann im nächstem Produktionshergang ausgeschmolzen wird.

Ein weiches Aluminiumnegativ wird von einem einzigen Messing Original hergestellt. Dies wird dann so oft mit Wachs gefüllt, wie es die Herstellung individueller Modelle erfordert. Jedes der Modelle wird dann in Keramik eingetaucht, die sich zur Form erhärtet. Anschließend wir der Wachs ausgeschmolzen, und die Formen zum Herstellen der Komponenten mit geschmolzenem rostfreiem Stahl gefüllt.

Der Wachsausschmelzguß ist eine traditionelle Technik, die auch heute noch bei der Herstellung von künstlichen Hüftgelenken angewandt wird. In diesem Prozeß entsteht eine abschließende Oberfläche, und hat darüberhinaus eine größere Genauigkeit als Sandguß. Dies, und die Tatsache, daß rostfreier Stahl länger hält und leichter renoviert werden kann, trägt zur hohen Wirtschaftlichkeit des Prozesses bei.

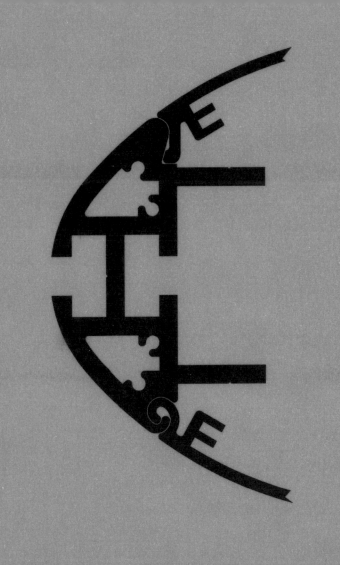

Los brazos que soportan el acristalado de la marquesina de autobús son fabricados empleando un proceso de fundición a cera perdida. Cada uno de los componentes es fabricado a partir de un único molde en cera que es entonces derretida o 'perdida' durante la siguiente etapa de producción.

Un negativo de aluminio blando se fabrica a partir de un maestro en bronce. Luego éste se rellena de cera las veces que sean necesarias para crear patrones individuales. A continuación cada uno de estos patrones se sumerge en un baño cerámico que al secarse y endurecerse forma un molde. Después la cera se derrite y el molde se rellena con acero inoxidable fundido para formar los componentes terminados.

La fundición a cera perdida es una técnica tradicional todavía utilizada hoy en día en la fabricación de prótesis para las articulaciones de cadera. El proceso no necesita un acabado y es capaz de conseguir mayor precisión que el proceso de fundición en arena. Esto, junto con el hecho de que el acero inoxidable es de máxima duración y fácilmente renovable, hace que el proceso sea muy económico.

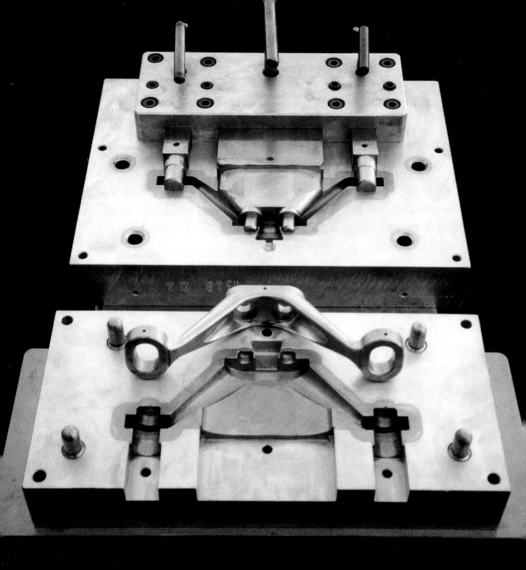

Tool for making waxes, with brass
master of glazing arm. Ceramic
coating of wax tree.

Pouring the stainless steel, cooling
and removal of ceramic residue.
Glazing arm detail.

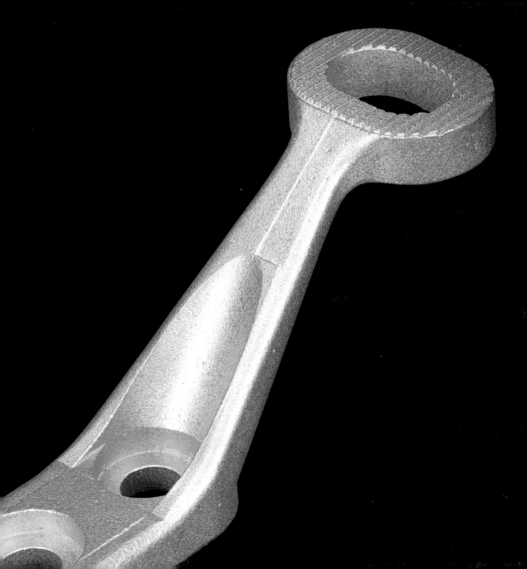

Signage is often the last aspect of a building to be considered. Expedient and ad hoc signage solutions often detract from a finished building.

German sign manufacturers Mabeg identified this problem as a potential gap in the market and commissioned Nicholas Grimshaw & Partners to develop a unified approach to signage specification. Their concept of signage is one which embraces all aspects of public information and orientation to provide a universally applicable and highly specifiable product. The key to this system is an extruded anodised aluminium track which can reliably accommodate every aspect of information display from glass signs to flat screen video monitors.

This universal fixing system can be fixed to walls or incorporated as part of a partition. Ideally the fixing system would be introduced into a building at an early stage to provide integrated signage for the exterior and interior. It can be integrated into a fixed item of furniture such as a reception desk. If installed as a door side product it can accommodate a range of accessories such as light switches and entry systems.

Die Beschilderung ist oft der letzte Aspekt, der bei einem Gebäude in Betracht gezogen wird, und Beschilderungsnotlösungen lenken oft von einem fertigen Gebäude ab.

Der deutsche Schildhersteller Mabeg identifizierte dieses Problem als eine potentielle Marktlücke, und beauftragte Nicholas Grimshaw & Partners mit der Entwicklung eines einheitlichen Verfahrens zur Beschilderungsspezifikation. Dieses Beschilderungskonzept ist eins, das alle Aspekte der Öffentlichkeitsinformation und Orientierung umfaßt, und stellt damit ein universell geeignetes und höchst spezifizierbares Produkt dar. Schwerpunkt dieses Systems ist eine im Strangpreßverfahren hergestellte, anodisierte Aluminiumschiene, die verläßlich für alle Aspekte der Informationsanzeige, von Glasschildern bis zu Flachbildvideomonitoren, benutzt werden kann.

Dieses Universalbefestigungssystem kann an Wänden angebracht, oder als Komponente einer Trennwand eingebaut werden. Zur Integration externer und interner Beschilderung baut man das Befestigungssystem idealerweise frühzeitig in das Gebäude ein. Es kann in ein festes Möbelstück, wie zum Beispiel einen Empfangstisch, eingebaut werden. Wenn es als Türseitenprodukt installiert ist, kann es eine Reihe von Zubehör halten, wie zum Beispiel Lichtschalter und Zutrittssysteme.

La señalización es a menudo el último aspecto a considerar en un inmueble. Las soluciones de señalización rápidas y concebidas sobre la marcha a menudo desmerecen el inmueble terminado.

El fabricante alemán de señalización Mabeg identificó este problema como un vacío potencial en el mercado y encargó a Nicholas Grimshaw & Partners el desarrollo de un planteamiento uniforme hacia la especificación de señalización. Su concepto de señalización comprende todos los aspectos de información y orientación pública para proporcionar un producto universalmente aplicable y cuya especificación resulta muy atractiva.

La clave de este sistema es una barra de aluminio extruído y anodizado capaz de adaptarse con fiabilidad a todos los aspectos de exhibición de información, desde letreros en cristal hasta monitores de vídeo de pantalla plana.

Este método universal de montaje puede instalarse en tabiques o incorporarse como parte de una división interna. La situación ideal es introducir el sistema de montaje en una etapa inicial de la construcción de un inmueble para proporcionar una señalización integrada tanto en el interior como en el exterior. Puede ser integrado en un artículo fijo de mobiliario tal como una mesa de recepción. Cuando se instala como producto en el lateral de una puerta puede incorporar una gama de accesorios tales como interruptores de alumbrado y sistemas de verificación de entrada.

The sign profile connection.
Profile One track.

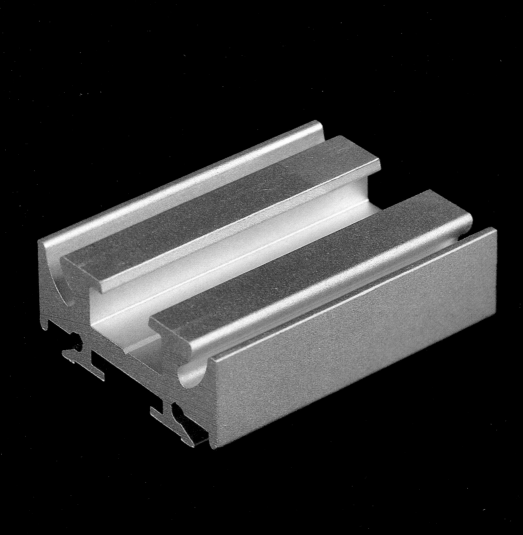

Profile One reception desk,
and integrated glazed partitions.

Signage has a significant role to play in the continuous expression of corporate identity, although most signage systems on the market offer little in the way of graphic flexibility.

This system developed for Mabeg provides a coherent but relatively anonymous standard which concentrates on the presentation of information, rather then the information itself.

The standard sign is a glass one, providing a transparent basis which can accommodate a number of graphic solutions. A panel of any material slotted between the two glass panels gives a maximum of six surfaces. Graphics can be layered, printed or etched, using any material in any combination.

*Die Beschilderung spielt beim Ausdruck der Firmenidentität ständig eine
bedeutende Rolle, trotzdem bieten die meisten marktgängigen Systeme wenig
grafische Flexibilität.*

*Dieses für Mabeg entwickelte System bietet einen zusammenhängenden,
aber relativ anonymen Standard, der sich auf die Präsentation der Information
statt auf die Information selber konzentriert.*

*Das Standardschild besteht aus Glas; es bietet somit eine durchsichtige
Basis, auf der eine Anzahl von Grafiklösungen unterbracht werden können. Ein
Platte aus beliebigem Material, zwischen den zwei Glasplatten eingeschoben,
ergibt ein Maximum von sechs Oberflächen. Grafiken können in allen Materialien
und allen Kombinationen geschichtet, gedruckt oder geätzt werden.*

La señalización juega un papel significante en la expresión continua de la
identidad corporativa, aunque la mayoría de los sistemas de señalización ofrecen
muy poca flexibilidad gráfica.

Este sistema, desarrollado para Mabeg, ofrece un estándar coherente pero
relativamente anónimo que centra su atención en la presentación de la
información en vez de la propia información.

El rótulo estándar es de cristal, lo cual ofrece una base transparente capaz de
adaptarse a una variedad de soluciones gráficas. Un panel de cualquier material
deslizado entre las dos hojas de cristal ofrece un máximo de seis superficies. Los
gráficos pueden ser escalonados, impresos o grabados, empleando cualquier
material en cualquier tipo de combinación.

Sign system mounted to Profile One
and to the Mast extrusion.

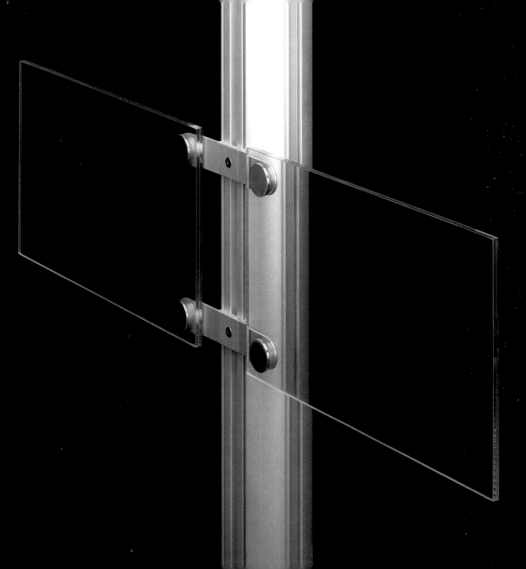

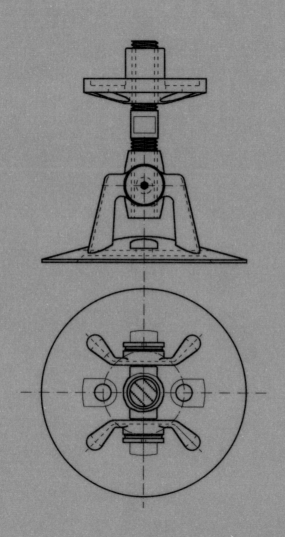

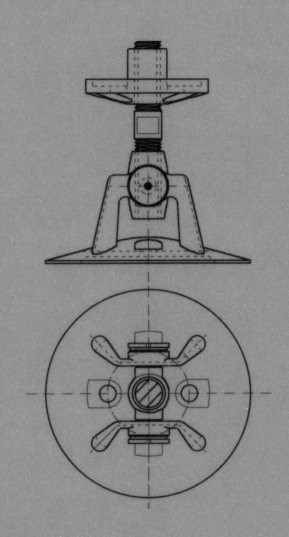

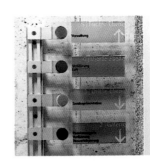

Essen Design Zentrum;
suspended, outdoor, exhibition
and directional signs

The design concept for this signage system centres around a kit of parts. It represents, for the manufacturer, an investment in a quality product designed to be compatible with high quality architecture.

With graphics becoming an increasingly significant aspect of company branding, signage becomes very important for a company intent on defining its identity. NGP's approach to signage recognises that flexibility is of paramount importance to the specifier. Given that a building is likely to be fitted out at least once every five years, the flexibility and quality of this system means it is more likely to be adapted than scrapped, and therefore will survive many cycles of refurbishment.

The range of these particular components means that both specifier and user can rely on a guaranteed minimum standard before they even begin to explore the possibilities of special additions and customising options. The fixing system itself is adaptable to the use of new technology, with signage embracing all aspects of orientation and the dissemination of information.

Mabeg's belief that "you never get a second chance at a first impression" is reflected in their desire to integrate this system into a building as early as possible.

Das Designkonzept für dieses Beschilderungssystem ist ein Teilebausatz, der für den Hersteller eine Investition in ein mit hochqualitiativer Architektur kompatibles Qualitätsprodukt darstellt.

Da Grafiken immer bedeutender für die Firmenselbstdarstellung werden, wird die Beschilderung für Firmen, die bewußt ihre Identität definieren wollen, sehr wichtig. NGP's Beschilderungsansatz erkennt an, daß für den Kunden die Flexibilität von überwältigender Wichtigkeit ist. Davon ausgehend, daß ein Gebäude wahrscheinlich mindestens einmal alle fünf Jahre neu ausgestattet wird, bedeutet die Flexibilität dieses Systems, daß es viel wahrscheinlicher angepaßt als verschrottet wird, und daher mehrere Renovierungszyklen überdauert.

Das Sortiment dieser speziellen Komponenten bedeutet, daß sich sowohl Planer als auch Benutzer auf einen garantierten Minimumstandard verlassen können, sogar bevor sie die Option der spezieller Zusätze und kundenspezifische Möglichkeiten erkunden. Das Anbringungssystem selber kann auf neue Technologien hin angepaßt werden, wobei die Beschilderung alle Aspekte der Ausrichtung, und die Verbreitung von Informationen umfaßt.

Mabegs Glaube daß "man niemals eine zweite Chance einen ersten Eindruck zu machen" erhält, spiegelt sich in ihrem Wunsch, das System so früh wie möglich in ein Gebäude zu integrieren, wieder.

El concepto del diseño para este sistema de señalización se centra en un juego de componentes y representa para el fabricante una inversión en un producto de calidad diseñado para ser compatible con la arquitectura de alta calidad.

Ya que los gráficos están siendo un aspecto cada día más importante de la imagen de las empresas, la señalización resulta muy importante para una compañía que se propone definir su identidad. El planteamiento de NGP sobre la señalización reconoce que la flexibilidad es de suma importancia para el licitante. Dado que un inmueble tiene probabilidad de ser rehabilitado por lo menos una vez cada cinco años, la flexibilidad y calidad de este sistema implica que es muy posible que sea adaptado y no desechado, y por ello continuará en servicio durante muchos ciclos de rehabilitación.

La gama de estos componentes específicos implica que tanto licitantes como los usuarios pueden confiar en un estándar mínimo garantizado antes incluso de comenzar a explorar las posibilidades de adiciones especiales y opciones de personalización disponibles. El propio sistema de fijación se adapta al empleo de nueva tecnología, con una señalización que comprende todos los aspectos de orientación y diseminación de información.

La creencia de Mabeg de que "nunca hay una segunda oportunidad para crear una primera impresión" está reflejada en su deseo de integrar este sistema en un inmueble lo más pronto posible.

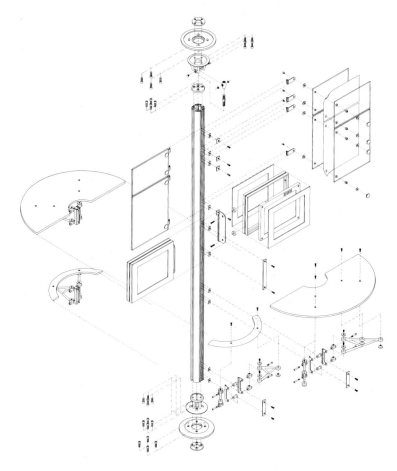

Kit of parts exploded. Mast assembly
with arms and table top.

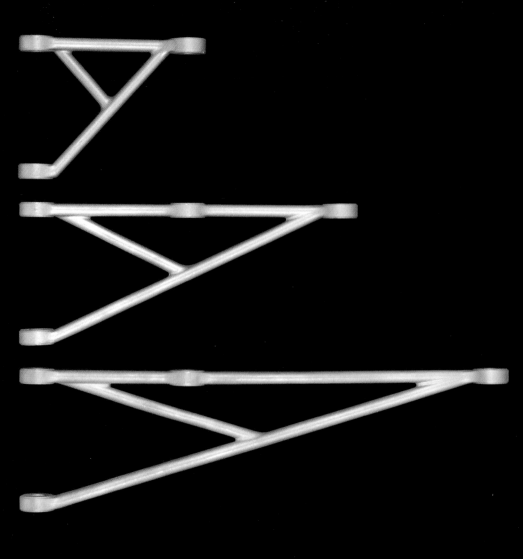

125, 250 and 375mm arms.

The Mabeg information mast is a stand alone product compatible with the signage range and combines the potential for both static and dynamic display. The extrusion for the mast contains the conduits for power and data cabling and can therefore display information in its widest sense. Animations, graphics, three dimensional orientation and an ability to be interrogated by the user are all possibilities.

As a product, the information mast anticipates the future of the signage market and attempts to meet the demands posed by world-wide and speech free communications.

The global exchange of key data, virtual banking for example, will be possible with individual organisations able to display or communicate their most important information via a dedicated location and in a co-ordinated way.

Der Mabeg Informationsmast ist ein Stand-alone Produkt, das mit der Beschilderungsserie kompatibel ist, und die Möglichkeiten für statische wie auch dynamische Anzeigen kombiniert. Die Strangpreßform für den Mast enthält den Kanal für die Strom– und Datenverkabelung, und kann daher Informationen im weitesten Sinne anzeigen. Animationen, Grafiken, dreidimensionale Ausrichtung und die Fähigkeit zur Benutzerabfragung sind alles Möglichkeiten.

Als ein Produkt weist der Informationsmast auf die Zukunft der Beschilderung und des Informationsmarktes hin, und versucht, den Forderungen der weltweiten und sprachenlosen Kommunikation gerecht zu werden.

Der globale Austausch von Schlüsseldaten, zum Beispiel der virtuelle Bankverkehr, wird ermöglicht, wobei einzelne Unternehmen in der Lage sind, ihre wichtigsten Informationen über eine dafür vorgesehene Position auf koordinierte Art und Weise anzuzeigen oder mitzuteilen.

El mástil informativo de Mabeg es un producto autónomo compatible con la gama de señalización y combina el potencial para la exposición tanto estática como dinámica. La extrusión del mástil contiene los conductos para cableado de suministro eléctrico y de datos, y puede por tanto exponer información en su sentido más amplio. Las animaciones, los gráficos, la orientación tridimensional además de una capacidad de ser interrogado por el usuario son todas posibilidades.

A nivel de producto, el mástil informativo anticipa el futuro del mercado de señalización e información e intenta alcanzar las exigencias planteadas por la comunicación global y de datos.

El intercambio global de información clave, por ejemplo las operaciones bancarias virtuales, será posible ya que las organizaciones individuales podrán exponer o comunicar su información más importante a través de un local dedicado y de una manera coordinada.

Mast with fixed signs, interactive
screen and table top. Mast extrusion.

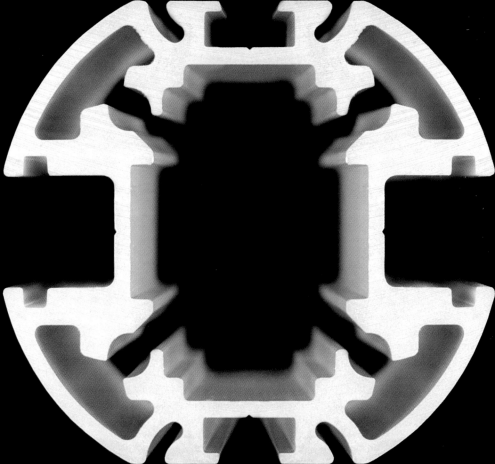

Foot rest and fixed foot. Single masts,
double masts with plasma screen
and external sign.

This door handle was initially developed for Nicholas Grimshaw and Partners' new Berlin Stock Exchange. It later came to be included in FSB's Berlin Range; a series of products designed for a new unified Berlin. Door furniture can be the first point of physical contact with a building. This design attempts to find the correct balance between form and function. A basic lever handle was worked out in model form to refine ideas that were ergonomically comfortable.

Aluminium castings and black plastic injection mouldings are bolted together with stainless steel screws. These materials create a visual contrast between heavy and light. The combination also emphasises a tactile contrast between cold metal and the thermoplastic grip which is warm to the touch. It is hoped, in due course, to offer alternative facing materials such as timber. The 'paddle' shape was initially inspired by the idea that a door should be easy to open by the elderly or by people with poor 'grip'. The intention was that they could simply rest their hand on the handle and, with very little downward pressure, the door would open.

Diese Türklinke wurde ursprünglich für Nicholas Grimshaw & Partners neue Berliner Börse entwickelt. Später wurde sie in die FSB Berlin-Serie mit aufgenommen; eine für das wiedervereinigte Berlin konzipierte Produktreihe. Das Türzubehör kann den Punkt des ersten körperlichen Kontaktes mit einem Gebäude darstellen. Dieses Design versucht ein Gleichgewicht zwischen Form und Funktion zu finden. Für ergonomische Bequemlichkeit wurde ein einfacher Türdrücker in Modellform ausgearbeitet.

Aluminiumgüsse und schwarze Einspritzformen aus Kunststoff werden mit Schrauben aus rostfreiem Stahl verschraubt. Diese Materialien stellen einen visuellen Kontrast zwischen Schwere und Leichtigkeit her. Die Kombination betont außerdem einen fühlbaren Kontrast zwischen kaltem Metall und dem thermoplastischen, sich warm anfühlenden Griff. Man hofft, daß man im Laufe der Zeit alternative Verkleidungen anbieten kann, wie zum Beispiel Holz. Inspiriert wurde die 'Paddelform' ursprünglich vom Gedanken, daß eine Tür von älteren Menschen, oder Menschen mit schwachem 'Griff' leicht zu öffnen sein sollte. Es wurde beabsichtigt, daß sie einfach ihre Hand auf den Griff auflegen könnten, und die Tür sich mit nur leichtem Druck nach unten öffnen läßt.

Esta manilla de puerta fue inicialmente concebida para la nueva Sede de la Bolsa de Berlín de Nicholas Grimshaw & Partners. Posteriormente, apareció incluida en la Serie Berlín de FSB, una serie de productos diseñados para el nuevo Berlín unificado. La ferretería puede ser el primer punto de contacto físico con un inmueble. Este diseño intenta encontrar el equilibrio correcto entre forma y función. Una manilla de palanca básica fue proyectada como prototipo para refinar las ideas de confort ergonómico.

Las piezas de aluminio de fundición y las molduras plásticas negras de inyección se montan juntas con tornillos de acero inoxidable. Estos materiales crean un contraste visual entre lo ligero y lo pesado. La combinación también resalta un contraste táctil entre el metal frío y la empuñadura termoplástica templada al tacto. Se espera en un futuro ofrecer materiales alternativos de acabado como la madera. La forma de 'paleta' fue inicialmente inspirada por la idea de que una puerta debería ser abierta con facilidad por los ancianos y por personas con poca fuerza en la mano. La intención era que estas personas sencillamente reposasen su mano sobre la manilla y con muy poca presión hacia abajo la puerta se abriese.

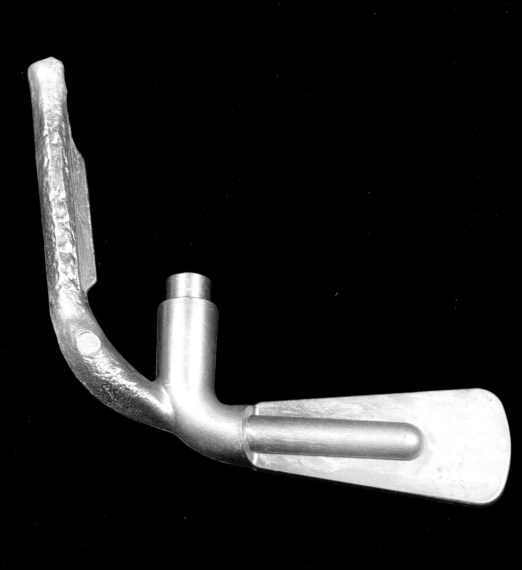

Matt, I'm still keen on the paddle shape (or golf club) I feel it would be nice to handle. surfaces could be wood or plastic with ss. core.

20/10/94.

Gravity die cast aluminium
door handle in production.
Overleaf, gravity die cast tool

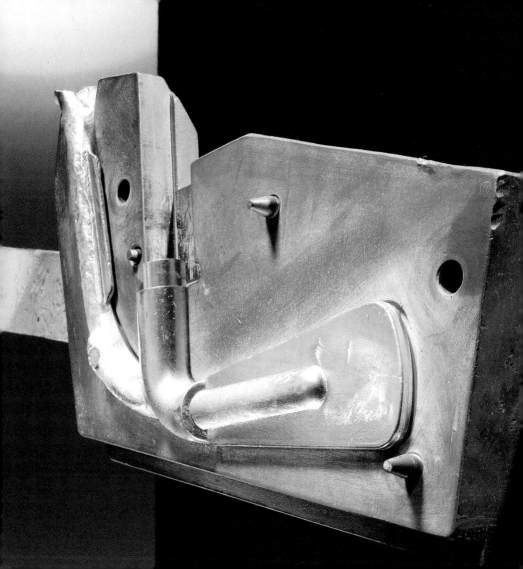

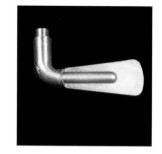  

Fettled, machined, polished
and finished handle.

The RAC Regional Control Centre in Bristol was designed as a landmark building for a national motoring organisation. The brief included the provision of overhead lighting for three floors of open plan office accommodation, serviced through a raised floor rather than via suspended ceilings.

Unusually, the lighting was an integral part of the overall design, developed from the outset in conjunction with the architectural structure of the building. The results of an early collaboration between architect and industrial designer are reflected in a solution which addresses both practical and aesthetic issues.

The extra ceiling height was used in the development of a suspended uplighting system providing an even, diffused light level of 300 lux at desk height. A slender central boom is suspended from the concrete structural beams on stainless steel rods, off which arms and luminaires are cantilevered. The luminaires reflect off specially formed coffers that soften the light and reduce glare for VDU users. A timing device contributes to energy conservation as well as providing flexibility for the user. The lighting booms and luminaires are manufactured from 1mm sheet steel and assembled off site. Only ceiling fixings and connections to the power supply are required.

Das Regionale Kontrollzentrum des RAC (Royal Automobile Club) in Bristol wurde als ein Wahrzeichengebäude für diesen nationalen Automobilverein konzipiert. Der Auftrag enthielt die Beschaffung von Deckenbeleuchtung für drei Etagen von Großraumbüros, mit Installation und Wartung über einen Doppelboden anstatt mittels einer untergehängten Decke.

Ungewöhnlicherweise war die Beleuchtung ein integraler Bestandteil des Gesamtdesigns, der von vorne herein im Zusammenhang mit der architektonischen Struktur des Gebäudes entwickelt wurde. Die Ergebnisse dieser frühen Zusammenarbeit zwischen Architekt und industriellem Designer spiegeln sich in einer Lösung wider, die sowohl praktische als auch ästhetische Belange berücksichtigt.

Die zusätzliche Deckenhöhe wurde in der Entwicklung eines hängenden Aufstrahlersystems ausgenutzt, das in Tischhöhe ein gleichmäßiges Streulicht von 300 Lux ermöglicht. Von den strukturellen Betonbalken hängt eine schlanke, zentrale Beleuchtungsschiene an Stäben aus rostfreiem Stahl, an welcher die Halterungen und Leuchtkörper einseitig eingespannt sind. Die Beleuchtungskörper werden von speziell geformten Deckenkassetten reflektiert, die das Licht weicher machen und es für Bildschirmbenutzer abblenden. Ein Zeitmechanismus trägt zum Energiesparen bei, und bietet zusätzliche Benutzerflexibilität. Die Beleuchtungsschienen und -körper werden aus 1mm dickem Stahlblech hergestellt, und werden außer Haus montiert. Nur die Deckenhalterungen und Anschlüsse zur Stromversorgung werden benötigt.

El Centro Regional de Control del Real Automóvil Club (RAC) en Bristol fue diseñado como un inmueble singular para una organización nacional automovilística. Los requisitos del edificio incluían la provisión de alumbrado en los techos de tres plantas de oficinas abiertas, con las instalaciones accesibles en los suelos técnicos en lugar de los falsos techos.

Singularmente, el alumbrado fue una parte integral del diseño global, desarrollado desde un principio junto con la estructura arquitectónica del edificio. Los resultados de una colaboración inicial entre el arquitecto y el diseñador industrial están reflejados en una solución en la que se consideran los aspectos prácticos y estéticos.

La altura adicional hasta el techo fue utilizada para concebir un sistema suspendido de focos bañadores de techo que ofrece un nivel de iluminación difusa de 300 lux a la altura de los escritorios. Un puntal central fino se suspende de las vigas de hormigón estructural por barras de acero inoxidable, de las cuales se proyectan brazos y luminarias extendidos en voladizo. Las luminarias se reflejan en cofres especialmente formados que suavizan el tono y reducen los reflejos para los usuarios de monitores de ordenador. Un dispositivo temporizador contribuye a la conservación de energía además de ofrecer flexibilidad al usuario. Los puntales del alumbrado y las luminarias están ambos fabricados en hoja de acero de 1 mm y se montan en fábrica. Sólo se requieren entonces los anclajes para techos y las conexiones para el suministro eléctrico.

South elevation and entrance bridge.

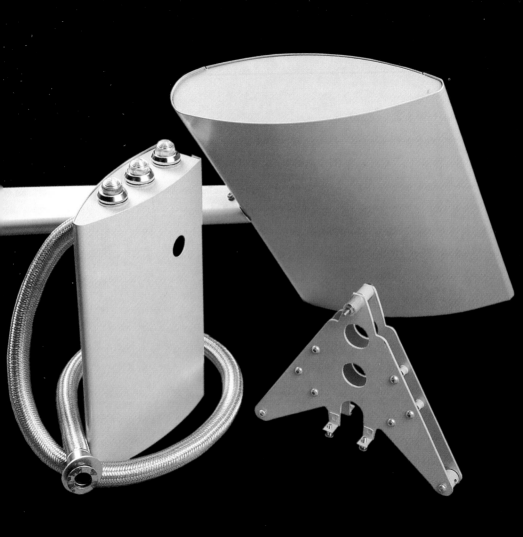

Lighting boom components
and installation.

This telephone installation at Waterloo International Terminal, developed for British Rail Telecom, was designed to provide a site which would enable different telephone network operators to locate their handsets. The base design is specific neither to the handset nor to its location and can be installed at any railway station.

The configuration of the assembly was determined by the need to minimise the space used on the site. The posts are the main structural element, providing support for both the telephones and the glass screens that separate them. The core of the post is a galvanised steel structure which houses power and data cables. The case is clad in satin polished stainless steel panels. Handsets can be fixed to the posts at any height, allowing for disabled users.

The glass screens were designed to solve spatial problems and provide the user with as much protected space as possible. They were manufactured from 10mm toughened glass and curved to create an 'S' shape. This special curvature meant that the glass was bent beyond the limits of standard techniques, and in two directions at the same time. All this was achieved using a vertical furnace with horizontal clamping. Both the technology and tool design were adapted from the automotive industry.

Diese, für British Rail Telecom entwickelte, Telefoneinrichtung am Internationalen Terminal Waterloo, wurde entworfen, um verschiedenen internationalen Telefonnetzbetreibern das Aufstellen ihrer Geräte zu ermöglichen. Das Basisdesign ist weder Gerät- noch ortspezifisch, und kann auf jedem beliebigen Bahnhof installiert werden.

Die Konfiguration der Montage wurde von der Notwendigkeit der Minimierung des Platzbedarfs vor Ort bestimmt. Die Säulen, die sowohl die Telefone, wie auch die sie trennenden Glasabschirmungen tragen, stellen das Hauptstrukturelement dar. Der Kern der Pfosten ist eine verzinkte Stahlstruktur, die die Strom– und Datenkabel enthält. Das Gehäuse ist mit seidenglatt polierten, rostfreien Stahlpaneelen verkleidet. Die Telefone können in beliebiger

Höhe am Pfosten angebracht werden, und tragen so den Belangen
körperbehinderter Benutzer Rechnung.
Die Glasabschirmungen wurden entwickelt, um räumliche Probleme zu lösen,
und dem Benutzer so viel geschützten Platz wir nur möglich zu geben. Sie wurden
aus 10mm starkem gehärtetem Glas hergestellt, und zur S-Form gekrümmt. Diese
spezielle Krümmung bedeutete, daß das Glas über die Grenzen der
Standardtechniken hinaus, und in zwei Richtungen gleichzeitig, gekrümmt wurde.
All dies wurde mit Hilfe eines vertikalen Schmelzofens mit horizontaler
Klemmung erreicht. Sowohl Technologie, als auch Werkzeugdesign wurden aus
der Automobilindustrie hergeleitet und angepaßt.

Esta instalación telefónica en la terminal Internacional de Waterloo, realizada
para British Rail Telecom, fue diseñada para ofrecer un local capaz de acomodar
las cabinas de los distintos operadores de redes telefónicas. El diseño de la base
no es específico para un tipo de cabina ni para su ubicación y puede ser instalada
en cualquier estación ferroviaria.

La configuración del módulo fue determinada por la necesidad de reducir al
máximo el espacio empleado en la estación. El poste es el elemento estructural
principal, ofreciendo soporte tanto para las cabinas como para las pantallas
acristaladas que las separan. El núcleo del poste es una estructura de acero
galvanizado que contiene el cableado eléctrico y de datos. La caja está revestida
con paneles de acero inoxidable pulido y satinado. Los teléfonos pueden ser
instalados en el poste a cualquier altura, permitiendo su uso por personas
minusválidas.

Las pantallas acristaladas fueron diseñadas para resolver problemas
espaciales y ofrecer al usuario el mayor espacio protegido posible. Fueron
fabricadas en cristal templado de 10 mm y curvado para crear una forma en "S".
La curvatura especial necesitó doblar el cristal más allá de los límites de las
técnicas normales, y en dos direcciones al mismo tiempo. Todo esto fue
conseguido empleando un horno vertical con mordazas horizontales. Tanto la
tecnología como las herramientas fueron adaptadas de la industria del automóvil.

Glass heated, pressed into shape and
toughened. 'Jig' to check tolerance.

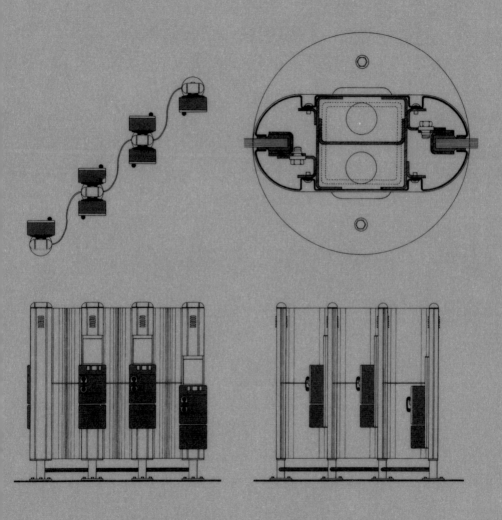

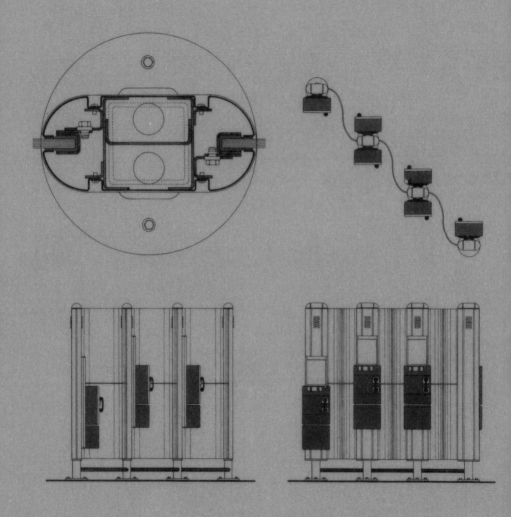

Telephones in departure area.
Base detail.

The cladding system designed for Igus GmbH factory and office development was based on a design used on the Herman Miller building at Chippenham ten years earlier.

The cladding system was designed to reflect the open, adaptable management structure of the company, and is therefore highly flexible.

The building consists of four blocks, each six by six bays. The external walls are composed of aluminium cladding panels fixed to standard Unistrut channels, reinforced to span the full height of the wall. Cladding panels are used to provide windows, doors and louvres. They are held in position by satin anodised aluminium clamps and can be easily interchanged. The interior face of the channels is used as a fixing point for fire hydrants, light switches, shelves and worksurfaces.

The furniture system is a kit of parts flexible and robust enough to provide standing and seated workstations for both the factory floor and the office areas.

Der Entwurf für des Verkleidungssystem des Igus GmbH Fabrik – und Büroprojektes basiert aut einem Entwurt der zehn Jahre vorher am Herman Miller Gebäude in Chippenham angewandt wurde.

Das Verkleidungssystem wurde so entwickelt, daß es die offene, anpassungsfähige Managementstruktur der Firma widerspiegelt; es ist damit äußerst flexibel.

Das Gebäude besteht aus vier Blöcken, jeder mit sechs mal sechs Feldern. Die Außenwände bestehen aus, an Standard Unistrebenkanälen befestigten Verkleidungspaneelen, so verstärkt, daß sie die gesamte Höhe der Wand abdecken. Verschiedene Verkleidungspaneele werden für Fenster, Türen und Jalousien benutzt. Sie werden von seidenmatten Klemmen aus eloxiertem Aluminium in Position gehalten, und können durch problemlos ausgetauscht werden. Die Innenfassade der Kanäle dient als Befestigungspunkt für Feuerhydranten, Lichtschalter, Regale oder Arbeitsflächen.

Das Möbelsystem besteht aus einem Einzelteilbausatz der flexibel und robust genug ist um Steh- und Sitzarbeitsplätze sowohl im Büro-als auch im Fabrikbereichen zu ermöglichen.

El sistema de revestimiento diseñado para la fábrica y desarrollo de oficinas de Igus GmbH se basó en un diseño utilizado diez años en el edificio de Herman Miller en Chippenham.

El sistema de revestimiento se fue diseñado para reflejar el estilo abierto y adaptable de la dirección de la compañía, y es por tanto altamente flexible.

El inmueble consiste en cuatro bloques, cada uno de seis por seis módulos. Los muros externos están construidos con paneles de revestimiento anclados a perfiles estándar Unistrut, reforzados para abarcar toda la altura del muro. Se utilizan paneles de revestimiento de distintos acabados y materiales para proporcionar ventanas, puertas y rejillas. Están anclados en su posición con abrazaderas de aluminio anodizado y pueden intercambiarse fácilmente. La superficie interior de los perfiles se emplea como punto de anclaje para bocas de incendios, interruptores de luz, estanterías o superficies de trabajo.

El sistema de mobiliario es un juego de componentes flexible y suficientemente robusto como para ofrecer estaciones de trabajo de pie y sentado en ambas áreas de oficina y taller.

Brake pressed aluminium panels
for Chippenham.

Igus cladding.

Igus furniture prototype, reception desk and factory interior.

The move of the Financial Times from Fleet Street to a key site in London's Docklands demanded a special response from Nicholas Grimshaw and Partners. The size and drama of the presses themselves suggested a transparent facade in order to exhibit the printing process to the passing public. The paper store and loading bay were enclosed in profiled aluminium panels creating the two solid ends of the building.

The glass facade is 92m long and 16m high consisting of 2m square panels of 12mm toughened glass bolted at each corner and sealed with silicon. The key glazing fixing detail consisted of a circular stainless steel plate, bolted through the glass at each four panel intersection to minimise visual interference.

Two metre long steel 'arms' welded from 16mm x 75mm steel bars hold the stainless steel plates in position and resist lateral wind loading. These arms are suspended by rods from the top of the aerofoil columns.

Fabricated steel aerofoil columns at 6m centres support the roof and the weight of the glass. The cladding for the paper store and loading bay consists of vacuum formed Superplastic aluminium panels.

Der Umzug der Financial Times von Fleet Street zu einer Schlüssellage in den London Docklands erforderte eine besondere Reaktion von Nicholas Grimshaw and Partners. Die Größe und Dramatik der Pressen selber legte eine transparente Fassade nahe, um den Druckvorgang für Passanten offenzulegen. Das Papierlager und die Ladebucht wurden von Formaluminiumpaneelen eingeschlossen, wodurch zwei feste Gebäudeecken geschaffen wurden.

Die Glasfassade ist 92m lang und 16m hoch, und besteht aus 2m² Paneelen aus 12mm gehärtetem Glas, die an den Ecken verschraubt und mit Silikon abgedichtet sind. Das Haupthalterungselement der Verglasung besteht aus einer runden Platte aus rostfreiem Stahl, die an jeder Vierpaneel-Schnittstelle durch das Glas verschraubt ist, was die visuelle Beeinträchtigung minimiert.

Zwei Meter lange, aus 16mm mal 75mm Stahlstangen geschweißte 'Stahlarme' halten die rostfreien Stahlplatten in Position und bieten Widerstand gegen Seitenwindbelastung. Diese Arme sind an Stangen von der Spitze der flügelförmigen Säulen heruntergehängt.

Vorgefertigte Flügelsäulen, mit 6m voneinander entfernten Mittelpunkten, stützen das Dach und das Gewicht des Glases. Die Verkleidung für das Papierlager und die Ladebucht besteht aus vakuumgeformten Superplastik-Aluminiumpaneelen.

La mudanza del periódico Financial Times desde Fleet Street a una localidad clave de la zona portuaria (Docklands) de Londres exigió un tratamiento especial por parte de Nicholas Grimshaw & Partners. El tamaño y dramatismo de las propias prensas clamaban una fachada transparente para exponer al transeúnte el proceso de imprenta rotativa. El almacén de papel y el área de carga y descarga se cubrieron con paneles de aluminio perfilado creando así los dos extremos sólidos del inmueble.

La fachada acristalada tiene 92 m de longitud y 16 m de altura con paneles de cristal templado de 2 metros cuadrados y 12 mm de espesor atornillados en cada esquina y sellados con silicona. El detalle clave de fijación del acristalado consistió en una placa circular de acero inoxidable, atornillada a través del cristal en cada intersección de 4 paneles para así reducir la interferencia visual.

'Brazos' de acero de dos metros de largo compuestos por barras de acero de 16 mm x 75 mm sostienen las placas de acero inoxidable en posición y resisten la carga lateral del viento. Estos brazos están suspendidos por varillas desde la parte superior de las columnas aerodinámicas.

Columnas aerodinámicas fabricadas con acero y centradas cada 6 metros soportan la cubierta y el peso del cristal. El revestimiento del almacén de papel y del área de carga y descarga consiste en paneles de aluminio Superplastic formados al vacío.

Corner panels and cladding detail.

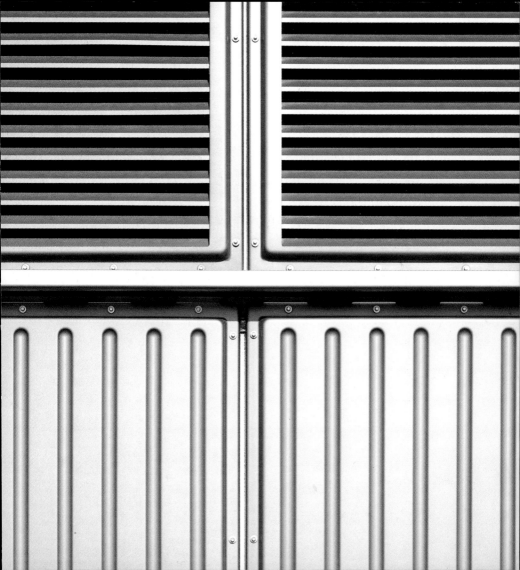

Planar glazing detail.

The Western Morning News headquarters nestles into a steeply sloping green field site and houses all the organisation's newspaper production, printing facilities and offices.

The skin of the building curves with the contours of the site resulting in a profile reminiscent of a ship. Concave glazed walls cut out sky reflections and allow spectacular views of the surrounding country. The design incorporates and develops many of the ideas first used on the Financial Times building.

The planar glazing is supported by a system of steel masts, cast ductile iron arms, cast brackets and adjustable stainless steel rods. The cast arms were the result of collaboration with Peter Rice of Ove Arup & Partners and his particular knowledge of spheroidal graphite. In its molten form it is less viscous than steel, allowing for finely detailed, slender castings. It adheres less to the sand used in the casting process, producing an improved surface finish. Spheroidal graphite is more economical than steel when casting relatively small pieces. Moulds of the arms are made via a timber pattern, the negative of which is used to create resin 'positives'.

The interface between every element in the glazing support assembly is designed to provide all necessary adjustments to accommodate both the angular change between the faceted glass panels and the associated constructional tolerances.

Die Zentrale der Western Morning News ist in eine sehr steile, grüne Wieselandschaft eingebettet, und enthält die gesamte Zeitungsproduktion des Unternehmens, sowie seine Druckmaschinen und seine Büros.

Die Gebäudehaut biegt sich in Nachahmung der Umgebung, was ein an ein Schiff erinnerndes Profil ergibt. Konkav verglaste Wände verhindern die Himmelsspiegelung und ermöglichen eine spektakuläre Aussicht auf das umgebende Land. Das Design beinhaltet und entwickelt viele der Ideen, die ursprünglich am Financial Times Gebäude benutzt wurden.

Die ebenflächige Verglasung wird von einem System aus Stahlmasten, nachgiebigen Gußeisentragstützen, Gußhalterungen und einstellbaren Stangen aus rostfreiem Stahl gestützt. Die Gußtragstützen waren das Ergebnis der Zusammenarbeit mit Peter Rice von Ove Arup & Partners, und dessen

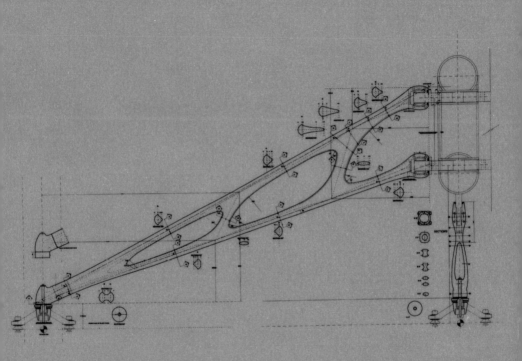

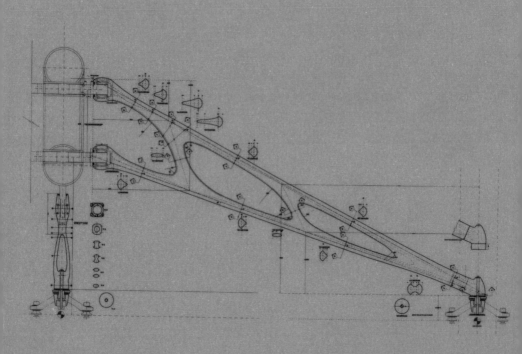

Spezialwissen über Kugelgraphit. In seiner geschmolzenen Form ist dieser
weniger viskos als Stahl, was die Herstellung sehr detaillierter, schlankerer
Gußformen erlaubt. Er haftet weniger am, beim Gußprozeß verwendeten Sand
an, und produziert so eine verbesserte Oberflächenbeschaffenheit. Wenn relativ
kleine Stücke zu gießen sind, ist Kugelgraphit wirtschaftlicher als Stahl. Formen
der Tragstützen werden mit Hilfe von Holzmustern hergestellt, deren Negative
zur Erstellung von Harz 'Positiven' verwendet werden.

Die Schnittstelle zwischen jedem Bauteil der Verglasungsstützenkonstruktion
ist so konzipiert, daß sie alle regulierenden Einstellungen ermöglicht, die nötig
sind, um sowohl die winkligen Veränderungen zwischen den facettierten
Glaspaneelen, als auch die nötigen baulichen Toleranzen zu ermöglichen.

La sede del diario Western Morning News está anidado en un campo verde en
pendiente muy aguda y contiene toda la producción del periódico, imprenta y
oficinas. El exterior del inmueble se curva con el entorno, lo que resulta en un
perfil que nos recuerda a un barco. Sus muros cóncavos acristalados eliminan los
reflejos del cielo y permiten vistas espectaculares del paisaje que lo rodea. El
diseño incorpora y pone en práctica muchas de las ideas empleadas por vez
primera en el inmueble del Financial Times.

El acristalado de tipo "Planar" está sostenido por un sistema de mástiles de
acero, brazos de hierro dúctil de fundición, soportes de fundición y varillas
ajustables de acero inoxidable. Los brazos de fundición fueron fruto de una
colaboración con Peter Rice de Ove Arup & Partners y su conocimiento específico
del grafito esferoide. En su estado líquido es menos viscoso que el acero y con él
se pueden obtener piezas fundidas finas y de alto detalle. También se adhiere
menos a la arena empleada en el proceso de fundición produciendo así un mejor
acabado en la superficie.

El grafito esferoide es más económico que el acero cuando se trata de
obtener piezas de fundición relativamente pequeñas. Los moldes para los brazos
se fabrican mediante un patrón de madera, cuyo negativo se emplea en la
producción de 'positivos' de resina.

El interface entre todos los elementos del conjunto de soporte para el
acristalado está ideado para proporcionar todos los ajustes que son necesarios
para aceptar tanto el cambio angular entre los paneles acristalados como las
tolerancias de construcción correspondientes.

 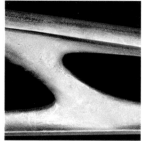 

Pattern and cast arms.

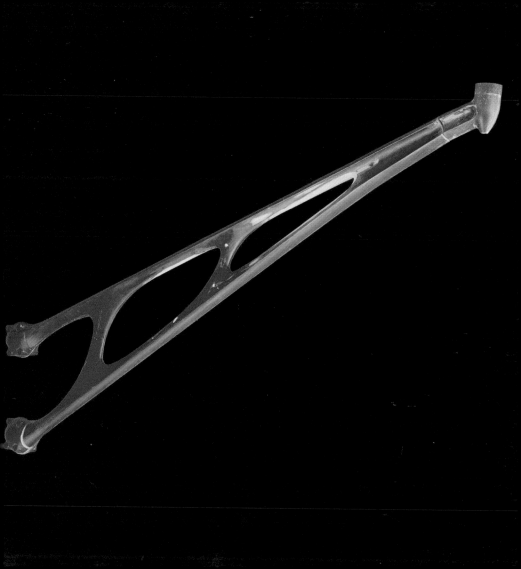

Tusk with glazing arms. Night view.

Designs for both Waterloo International Terminal and the British Pavilion at the Seville Expo in 1992 have developed ways of achieving sheer and transparent walls. At Waterloo, a glazed wall creates an environmental separation between the existing domestic terminal and the International Terminal. Full views of the spectacular station are made possible through the use of a slender self-supporting bow string detail which runs through the line of the glass itself creating a delicate and sheer elevation. The bow string has no structural function other than supporting the weight of the glass and dealing with horizontal wind loads. There are no vertical mullions or sills to interfere with visibility. The glazing boss was manufactured using a lost wax casting process.

The British Pavilion was built in Seville, Europe's hottest city. The east facade, through which the public entered consisted of a water-cooled glass curtain wall which created comfortable conditions as well as a spectacular first impression. Sheets of glass are fixed together by means of internal steel plates with bolts through the glass, and joints are sealed flush with silicon so that the whole wall is a single surface, with no projecting mullions or transoms to interrupt the flow of water. Glass panels were suspended one off another with the internal boom dealing with wind loading. Cascading water cooled and animated its entire surface. These techniques contributed to a demountable design which was pre-fabricated off site and erected in just under a year.

Bei den Entwürfen für das International Terminal Waterloo und den britischen Pavillon der Weltausstellung in Sevilla im Jahre 1992, wurden die Möglichkeiten, steile und transparente Wände zu erzielen, entwickelt. In Waterloo schafft eine Glaswand eine Umgebungsabgrenzung zwischen dem bestehenden Inlands– und dem internationalen Terminal. Freier Ausblick auf den spektakulären Bahnhof wird mit Hilfe eines schlanken, selbsttragenden Bogenträgerelementes erreicht, das durch die Glaslinie selber verläuft, und eine feine und steile Ansicht erschafft. Der Bogenträger hat, außer das Glasgewicht zu stützen, und mit der horizontalen Windbelastung fertigzuwerden, keine weitere strukturelle Funktion. Es gibt keine sichtbeeinträchtigenden Zwischenpfosten oder Simse. Der Verglasungsbossen wurde mittels eines Wachsausschmelzgußprozesses gefertigt.

Der britische Pavillon wurde in Sevilla, Europas heißester Stadt, gebaut. Die

Wand der Ostfassade, durch die das Publikum das Gebäude betrat, bestand aus einem wassergekühlten Glasvorhang, der sowohl angenehme Umweltbedingungen schaffte, als auch für einen spektakulären ersten Eindruck sorgte. Glasscheiben wurden mit Hilfe interner Stahlplatten mit Schrauben durch das Glas aneinander befestigt, die Fugen mit Silikon verdichtet, so daß die gesamte Wand eine einzige Oberfläche bildete, ohne daß herausragende Pfosten oder Riegel den Wasserfluß beeinträchtigten. Glasscheiben wurden voneinander herabgehängt, wobei der interne Ausleger für den Ausgleich der Windbelastung sorgte. Fallendes Wasser kühlte und animierte die gesamte Oberfläche. Diese Technik trug zu einem abmontierbaren Design bei, das fernab vorgefertigt, und in weniger als einem Jahr erbaut wurde.

En ambos diseños de la Terminal Internacional de Waterloo y del Pabellón Británico en la Exposición Mundial de Sevilla de 1992 se investigaron modos de conseguir muros diáfanos y transparentes. En Waterloo, un muro acristalado crea una separación medioambiental entre la terminal nacional existente y la Terminal Internacional. Las vistas completas de la espectacular estación son posibles mediante el uso de una fina cercha en aro de soporte autónomo que atraviesa la línea del acristalado creando así una fachada delicada y diáfana. La cercha en aro no tiene otro objeto que soportar el peso del cristal y neutralizar las cargas horizontales del viento. No hay parteluces ni antepechos que puedan interferir con la visibilidad. El tachón del acristalado se fabricó utilizando un proceso de fundición a cera perdida.

El Pabellón Británico se construyó en Sevilla, la ciudad más calurosa de Europa. La fachada este, por la cual hacía su entrada el público, consistía en un muro cortina acristalado refrigerado por agua creando condiciones agradables además de una primera impresión muy espectacular. Las hojas de cristal son montadas mediante placas internas de acero con tornillos que atraviesan el cristal, y las juntas se sellan a paño con silicona de modo que el muro entero constituye una única superficie, sin parteluces ni travesaños salientes que puedan interrumpir el flujo del agua. Los paneles se suspendían el uno del otro y la carga del viento se recogía en las barras internas. Las aguas en cascada refrigeraban y animaban la superficie entera del muro. Estas técnicas contribuyeron a concebir un diseño desmontable que fue prefabricado fuera de la obra e instalado en menos de un año.

View of Waterloo roof through
bow string truss glazed wall
and detail.

Pavilion water wall and interior view.

The interior spaces at Waterloo International Terminal are defined by the shape of the platforms and tracks above. The waiting areas have been located directly below the platforms to allow higher ceilings, while retail space is concentrated below the tracks where the ceilings are lower.

Variations in lighting further differentiate these areas. Downlighters, which draw attention to objects at lower levels, are used in the retail area. Uplighters are used in the waiting areas, to define and enhance the curvature of the space. The uplighting luminaires consist of three elements; light, boom and fixing bracket. A sand blasted aluminium casting forms the light itself. The boom consists of a long, hollow stainless steel tube, connected to the light by means of a small aluminium sand casting bolted to the light. The idea of a long boom means that the surface of the panels can be lit directly to emphasise the structure of the building. The assembly can be fixed onto the ceiling in such a way that the fixing bracket remains concealed in the junction between two of the ceiling panels.

Die Innenräume des internationalen Terminals Waterloo werden von der Form der darüberliegenden Bahnsteige und Gleise definiert. Um höhere Decken zu ermöglichen, wurde der Wartebereich direkt unterhalb der Bahnsteige angesiedelt, während der Verkaufsbereich unterhalb der Gleise konzentriert ist, wo die Decken niedriger sind.

Des weiteren differenziert unterschiedliche Beleuchtung zwischen den beiden Flächen. Abwärtsstrahler, die die Aufmerksamkeit auf Gegenstände in tieferen Ebenen lenken, kommen im Verkaufsbereich zum Einsatz. Aufstrahler werden im Wartebereich genutzt, wo sie die Raumkrümmung definieren und steigern. Die aufstrahlenden Beleuchtungskörper bestehen aus drei Elementen, dem Licht, der Beleuchtungsschiene und der Halterung. Die Lampe selber besteht aus sandgestrahltem Aluminiumguß. Die Beleuchtungsschiene besteht aus einem langen, hohlen Rohr aus rostfreiem Stahl, das mittels eines kleinen Aluminiumsandgußformstücks an die Lampe geschraubt ist. Die Idee einer langen Beleuchtungsschiene bedeutet, daß die Paneeloberflächen zur Betonung der Gebäudestruktur, direkt angestrahlt werden können. Die Konstruktion kann so an der Decke angebracht werden, daß die Halterung in der Verbindung zwischen zwei Deckenpaneelen verborgen ist.

Los espacios interiores de la Terminal Internacional de Waterloo están definidos por la forma de los andenes y las vías por encima de ellos. Las zonas de espera se ubicaron directamente por debajo de los andenes para obtener techos más altos, mientras que los espacios comerciales se concentran por debajo de las vías donde los techos son más bajos.

Las variaciones del alumbrado diferencian aún más estas zonas. Los focos bañadores de suelo, que enfocan objetos a niveles más bajos, se emplean en la zona comercial. Los focos bañadores de techo se emplean en las zonas de espera para definir y embellecer la curvatura del espacio. Las luminarias bañadoras de techo consisten en tres elementos: lámpara, barra y abrazadera de soporte. La lámpara en sí es una pieza de aluminio de fundición acabado con chorro de arena. La barra de suspensión consiste en un tubo largo y hueco de acero inoxidable, conectado a la propia lámpara mediante una pequeña pieza de aluminio de fundición en arena atornillada a la lámpara. La idea de una barra larga significa que la superficie de los paneles puede ser alumbrada directamente para resaltar la estructura del inmueble. El conjunto puede ser montado en el techo de tal manera que la abrazadera de soporte permanece oculta en la junta entre dos paneles del techo.

Placing of sand insert within main mould; cast luminaire casing and knuckle joint. Pattern for exterior of uplighter casing .

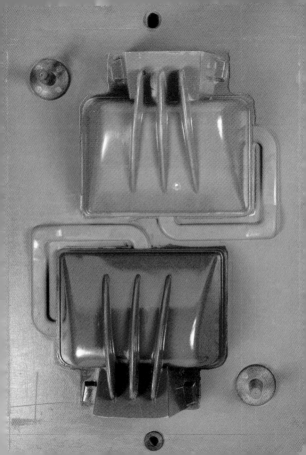

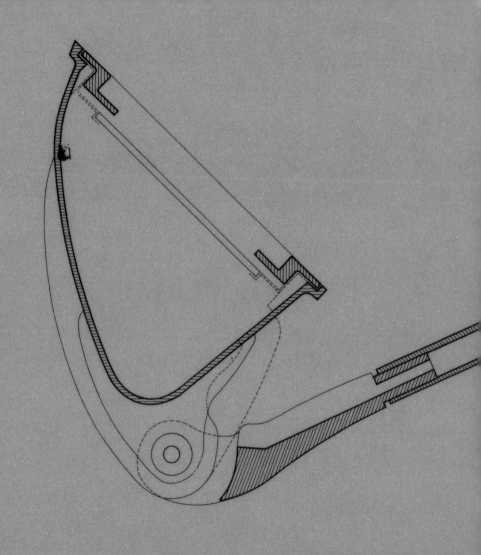

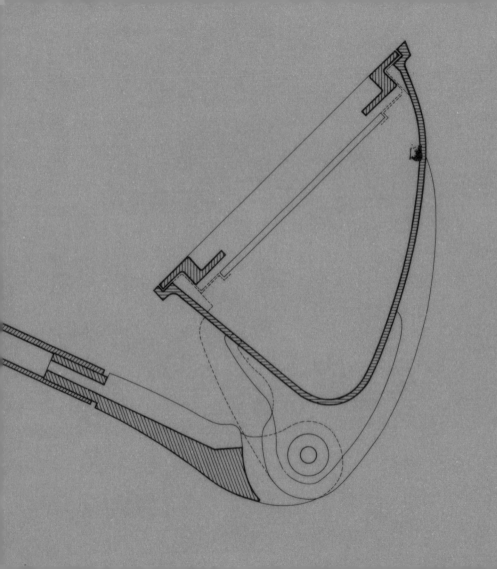

Uplighter in departures area. Detail of
cast lamp and reflector housing.

The glazed roof of the International Terminal at Waterloo is the focus of the project's technical achievements and architectural spectacle. Its transparency acts as a showcase for the Eurostar trains which operated a service from London to the rest of Europe for the first time in 1994. One effect of a constrained urban site was the complicated roof geometry whereby none of the arches are parallel or have the same span. A standard glazing system involving thousands of panels of different shapes and sizes would have been prohibitively expensive.

The solution was to adopt a 'loose fit' approach in which a limited number of panel sizes were used. Each one is held in a frame and overlaps at each end. The panels are laterally connected by neoprene gaskets which can expand to accommodate the varying width in plan. Individual components can easily be replaced. As a result the roof has a 125 year life span.

The mullions are connected to the glazing panel framing by an assembly of stainless steel castings. Over 2200 of these components were required in the length of the roof, which allowed Nicholas Grimshaw & Partners to experiment for the first time with lost wax casting as a means of casting production.

Das Glasdach des internationalen Terminals Waterloo ist der Fokus der technischen Leistungen des Projektes, und ein architektonisches Erlebnis. Seine Transparenz dient als Schaufenster für die Eurostar Züge, die im Jahre 1994 zum erstem Mal den Pendelverkehr zwischen London und anderen europäischen Großstädten aufnahmen. Eine Auswirkung der Lage im begrenzten Stadtgebiet war die komplizierte Dachgeometrie, wobei keiner der Bögen parallel zueinander verläuft, noch die gleiche Spannweite hat. Ein Standardverglasungssystem mit Tausenden von Paneelen unterschiedlicher Formen und Größen, wäre unverantwortbar teuer gewesen.

Die Lösung lag in einem Ansatz des 'Lockeren Sitzens', bei dem eine begrenzte Anzahl von Paneelgrößen genutzt wurde. Jedes davon wird in einem

Rahmen gehalten, und überschneidet an beiden Enden. Die Paneele sind seitlich durch Neoprendichtungen miteinander verbunden, die sich derart erweitern können, daß sie alle im Plan vorkommenden, unterschiedlichen Breiten aufnehmen können. Einzelne Komponenten sind leicht austauschbar. Das Dach hat daher eine Lebensdauer von 125 Jahren.

Die Pfosten sind durch eine Konstruktion von Gußformen aus rostfreiem Stahl mit den Glaspaneelrahmen verbunden. Über 2200 dieser Komponenten wurden in der Dachlänge benötigt, was es Nicholas Grimshaw & Partners erlaubte, zum ersten Mal mit Wachsausschmelzgießen als Mittel zur Gußformherstellung zu experimentieren.

La cubierta acristalada de la Terminal Internacional de Waterloo es el foco de atención de los éxitos técnicos y del propio espectáculo arquitectónico del proyecto. Su transparencia actúa como un escaparate para los trenes Eurostar que comenzaron su servicio desde Londres hacia el resto de Europa por vez primera en 1994. Uno de los efectos del solar urbano con limitaciones fue la complicada geometría de la cubierta en la que ninguno de sus arcos son paralelos o tienen el mismo vuelo. Un sistema estándar de acristalado que comprendiese miles de paneles de distintas formas y tamaños hubiera resultado extremadamente costoso.

La solución fue adoptar un planteamiento de 'componentes autónomos' en el que se emplearon un número limitado de tamaños de paneles. Cada uno de estos se sostiene en un marco y queda solapado en cada extremo. Los paneles están conectados lateralmente con juntas de neopreno que pueden dilatarse para aceptar la variación de anchura en la planta. Los componentes individuales pueden ser fácilmente sustituidos. En consecuencia, la cubierta tiene una vida útil de 125 años.

Los parteluces están conectados a los marcos de los paneles acristalados por un juego de piezas de fundición de acero inoxidable. Fue necesario utilizar más de 2200 de estos componentes en toda la longitud de la cubierta, lo cual permitió a Nicholas Grimshaw & Partners experimentar por primera vez con piezas de fundición a cera perdida como medio de producción.

The wax tree is coated in ceramic,
then melted out, and molten stainless
steel is poured into the mould.
From prototype to production.

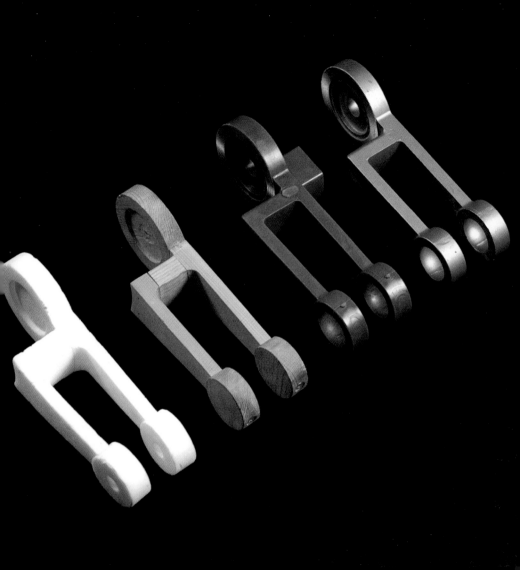

Interior view of roof.
Exploded computer rendering,
Glazing panel hangar. Night view.

The west wall at Waterloo forms a spatial link between the arrival and departure lounges as well as a double height drop off point at the side of the building. It provides a weatherproof barrier and allows natural light into the interior.

Located directly below the platform and track bed slab, the wall needed to be able to deflect with the vibration caused by the 800 tonne moving trains. The necessary displacement is achieved by a sophisticated glazing system which allows the entire wall to move in any one direction. It consists of a slider bar that holds the glazing panels at the top end and a series of glass fins that stiffen the wall on the inside. These fins are connected to the glazing panels by bracket assemblies to allow vertical and horizontal displacements of 60mm and 80mm respectively. The glazing panels are silicon jointed to cater for relative motion between them.

Both the slider bar and the brackets are stainless steel lost wax castings. The sliding rods are machined from stainless steel bars. The planar fittings are machined stainless steel.

Die Westwand in Waterloo stellt eine räumliche Verbindung zwischen den Ankunfts– und Abfahrtshallen her, sowie einem zweigeschössigen Anlieferungs– und Abholpunkt zur Seite des Gebäudes. Sie bietet eine wettergeschützte Barriere und läßt Tageslicht ins Innere.

Direkt unter der Bahnsteig– und Gleisbettplatte angesiedelt, mußte die Wand in der Lage sein, die, von 800 Tonnen schweren, fahrenden Zügen verursachten Schwingungen abzuleiten. Die nötige Verdrängung wird durch ein ausgeklügeltes Glassystem erreicht, das zuläßt, daß sich die gesamte Wand in jede beliebige Richtung bewegen kann. Es besteht aus einem Schiebebalken der die Glaspaneele am oberen Ende festhält, und einer Reihe von Glasrippen, die die Wand von der Innenseite versteifen. Diese Rippen sind mit Hilfe von

Halterungseinheiten an den Glaspaneelen befestigt, was vertikale und horizontale Verdrängungen von 60mm bzw. 80mm ermöglicht. Die Glaspaneele sind Silikonverfugt, um der relativen Bewegung zwischen ihnen Rechnung zu tragen.

Sowohl der Schiebebalken, als auch die Halterungen sind aus Wachsausschmelzgußformen aus rostfreiem Stahl. Die Gleitstangen wurden aus rostfreien Stahlstangen maschinell gefertigt. Die ebenen Beschläge sind aus maschinell gefertigtem rostfreien Stahl.

El muro oeste de Waterloo forma un enlace espacial entre las salas de llegadas y salidas, además de ser un punto de doble altura para el apeo de pasajeros en el lateral del inmueble. El muro proporciona una barrera contra la intemperie y permite la penetración de luz natural al interior.

Localizado directamente por debajo de la losa estructural de la plataforma y vías férreas, el muro necesitaba ser capaz de flexionarse con la vibración causada por el movimiento de los trenes de 800 toneladas. El desplazamiento se consigue por un sofisticado sistema de acristalamiento que permite el movimiento del muro entero en cualquier dirección. Consiste en una barra deslizante que sostiene los paneles acristalados por el extremo superior y una serie de alerones de cristal que refuerzan el muro por el interior. Estos alerones están conectados a los paneles acristalados por un sistema de soportes con el fin de permitir desplazamientos verticales y horizontales de 60 mm y 80 mm respectivamente. Los paneles acristalados están unidos mediante silicona para aceptar el movimiento relativo entre ellos.

Tanto la barra deslizante como los soportes son de acero inoxidable de fundición a cera perdida. Las varillas deslizantes están producidas usando barras de acero inoxidable maquinadas. Los accesorios de tipo "Planar" son de acero inoxidable maquinado.

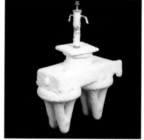
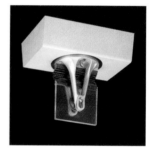

Wax tree, ceramic coated tree and
glazing hanger assembly.
Single wax hanger

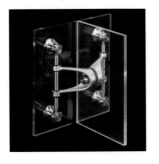

West wall glazing in arrivals.
Glazing 'spider' detail.

**Exhibition designed developed
and produced by**

142 ◼

Nicholas Grimshaw and Partners
Billings Jackson
MABEG Kreuschner GmbH & Co. KG
Zumtobel Staff GmbH

Exhibition sponsored by

CEMUSA (Corporación Europea de Mobiliario Urbano S.A)
BüroDesignCenterNänikon
Lista AG/Denz & Co. AG
Environmental Technology Ltd. (ENTECH)
Franz Schneider Brakel GmbH + Co. (FSB)
MABEG Kreuschner GmbH & Co. KG
Sean Billings Design Associates Ltd
Spagnol Luthi Associes S.A
Zumtobel Staff GmbH

Photographic credits

Alan Batham pp. 28, 29, 30, 31, 32, 33, 37, 38, 39, 42, 44,
    45, 46, 47, 53, 63, 64, 69, 70, 71, 75, 76, 80, 84, 85,
    127, 132, 133, 138, 139, 141
Peter Cook pp. 88, 91
Michael Dyer Associates pp. 90, 97
Frank Göldner pp. 56, 65 c+r
Katsuhisa Kida pp.89, 116
John Linden pp. 96, 104, 105, 120, 140
Jo Reid & John Peck pp.100, 101, 102, 103, 108, 109,
    110, 111, 117, 122, 123, 128, 134
Tim Soar p. 58
Peter Strobel pp. 114, 115, 121, 129, 135 c
Nigel Young p. 65L,

█ **143**

Other exhibits kindly contributed by

Alcasting, s.l
Commercial Systems International Ltd.
GIG Fassadenbau GmbH
Igus GmbH
Llama-Gabilondo Y CIA, S.A
MAG Hansen
MBC Precision Castings
Pilkington Architectural
R. Glazzard (Dudley) Ltd
Superform Aluminium

Computer Renderings

Trace Digital Art pp. 59, 62, 74, 77

First published in 1998 by
Nicholas Grimshaw and Partners
1 Conway Street
Fitzroy Square
London WC1P 6LR

ISBN 1–874044–26–0

A CIP catalogue record for this book is
available from the British Library.

Catalogue produced and distributed by
Art Books International, London.

Designed by Isambard Thomas.

Printed and bound by Grafiche Milani.